Everyone's Invited

Soma Sara

GALLERY BOOKS UK

First published in Great Britain by Gallery UK,
an imprint of Simon & Schuster UK Ltd, 2022

1 3 5 7 9 10 8 6 4 2

Simon & Schuster UK Ltd
1st Floor
222 Gray's Inn Road
London WC1X 8HB

www.simonandschuster.co.uk
www.simonandschuster.com.au
www.simonandschuster.co.in

Simon & Schuster Australia, Sydney
Simon & Schuster India, New Delhi

A CIP catalogue record for this book is available from the British Library

Hardback ISBN: 978-1-3985-1485-0
eBook ISBN: 978-1-3985-1486-7

Typeset in Bembo by
Palimpsest Book Production Ltd, Falkirk, Stirlingshire
Printed in the UK by CPI Group (UK) Ltd, Croydon, CR0 4YY

Please be mindful that these essays contain themes that may be triggering to the reader. There are mentions and references to sexual harassment, sexual abuse, assault, rape, domestic abuse and violence, image-based sexual harassment and abuse, eating disorders, suicide ideation and suicide.

Although these essays frequently centre around heterosexual experiences, *Everyone's Invited* is proudly LGBTQ+ inclusive. For more information about LGBTQ+ experiences please refer to the charities listed on the Everyone's Invited website.

Contents

Introduction

Growing up in London was exciting. As we hurtled towards adulthood, my friends and I explored a city of possibility. We ran around town from postcode to postcode, on the tops of double-decker buses, sweaty Tubes, and Barclays bikes, dancing in pubs, clubs, parks and in whoever's house was free over the weekend. The city felt unreal. A ripe sun, a white sky and the half-heartedness of London's rain. Yet there was always danger in a safe place. Danger that looks like a 'great guy' who is 'just a bit weird with girls'. Danger that feels like your friend who you thought you could trust. Danger in the lingering hand on the small of your back. Those disturbing little moments that wash over you as no big deal. But still, you moved, you ebbed, you flowed. You waded through the parties, the darkness of the clubs, between the drinks and the lakes of deepening and shallowing conversations. You got over the heartache, you laughed like lions with your friends, you picked each other up and borrowed each other's clothes, you felt alone in the emptiness of a crowded place. Wearing the heavy layers of arrogance and insecurity, the defining forces of teenagehood, you moved from north to south, from east to west; you embodied the city. You let it take you in its tide. You felt freedom. Never falling behind, always staying in tune, thrusting forward, onwards, you matched its energy, you kept up. It was all at once a reckoning of pace, of balance, of pulse. But you never paused, you never considered, you never stopped. You did not reflect on the dehumanising experiences you were having, the misogynistic behaviours you were normalising or the culture that framed it all. Unknowingly and unconsciously, those insidious moments that swung by like dreams are, in the end, the things that stayed deep within you. Those forgotten experiences, which lay dormant in your mind for years, are what profoundly shaped your life and the person you have become.

I had grown up attending all-girls schools and was raised by a single dad who fulfilled the roles of both mother and father. Messages of empowerment, confidence and self-belief had been embedded in me from a young age; I had a feminist grandmother, too. As a young child, I was taught that I could do anything and be anyone. The idea of my gender holding me back in any way was completely alien. When I was around the age of fourteen, I had a conversation with a boy at a house party that has stuck with me till this day. I was, for the first time, faced with a new reality. The more we spoke, the more I began to understand how my world view was radically different to his own. I will never forget when he asked me whether I believed in equality of the sexes and told me how, in his opinion, men were in body and mind naturally superior to women, citing Darwinism and evolution to justify these beliefs. I know this might seem small, but at the time I was genuinely shocked – I had been safeguarded and sheltered my entire life. I assumed that everyone thought how I thought and believed what I believed. It felt a little absurd; I remember almost laughing. But I was also disturbed by what he said, and by the fact that someone whom I considered a close friend viewed me as inferior to himself and his male peers.

The older I grew and the more I began to socialise, the more aware I became of 'inequality'. It edged increasingly into the world I was beginning to navigate, manifesting in many different ways throughout my teenage years and epitomised in the daily reality of street harassment. Older men asserted their power by shouting sexual and lewd comments, often accompanied by crude gestures.

Now, with hindsight, I realise that these experiences forced an acute awareness of my own physical appearance and body image, and imposed a non-consensual sexualisation of my prepubescent body. At the time, I was scared, but I just accepted it as part of what it meant to be a teenage girl.

As time passed, these moments of powerlessness became inherent to my daily life. Whether it was the derogatory ways that boys spoke about women and girls, the bragging about sexual conquests, the objectifying comments about female bodies, jokes about sexual harassment and sexual assault, or the slut shaming, this incremental dehumanisation had a profound impact on my self-worth, mental health and relationships. But despite all this, it was just seen as normal.

The London I grew up in was characterised by this culture. Over time, it had the cumulative effect of normalising and trivialising experiences of sexual violence. It was an insidious presence. Subtle yet powerful. Invisible but deeply felt. On reflection, and after many conversations with friends, there were so many moments that felt 'wrong', 'weird' or 'uncomfortable', but only with hindsight did we realise how destructive many of those experiences were. Growing up, misogyny, sexual harassment and sexual abuse online were normalised amongst my peers; libraries of nudes of underage girls were shared on Google drives, being groped and grabbed at a party was normal, as were the unwanted advances, rape jokes, sexual bullying and unsolicited dick pics. Boys received and girls gave. There was pressure to engage in sex acts; pressure that wasn't visible per se, or always clear as to where it came from at the time, but felt like a pre-established component of our existence.[1] In a world of sex without dating, where brutal double standards shamed girls as 'sluts' but rewarded boys for having sex, assaults were not rare. There were exorbitant pressures on young girls to perform 'hotness' online, not to mention the pornographic sexual script that dictated the real sex lives of young people. Porn was the wallpaper that framed our lives, normalising it all, and the status quo rarely challenged.[2] There were no words, no understanding, no frame of reference to effectively challenge what was happening. Without realising it, I was internalising a sense of self-blame that was cultivated by this environment. We were implicitly programmed to laugh off our discomfort and carry on. This was our normal; we believed it was 'just a part of life' and a 'part of growing up'. I believe that many of the perpetrators didn't understand what they were doing or the magnitude of their actions either.

I remember sometimes trying to challenge this behaviour, by objecting to being grabbed or being spoken to in a sexual way. But often I lacked an understanding of what was happening to me and how it might affect me in the long term, and I didn't know how to stop it. We were so young, naïve and impressionable, we didn't have the knowledge or the courage to effectively intervene or stand up for ourselves at the time. I wanted to be accepted, liked and loved – I wanted to take risks, have fun, explore life, learn and grow like any other teenage girl.

But we internalise these moments, and every experience, big or small, has an impact. This is what I've learnt from my own experiences and from the testimonies of others. In 2020, I created an online social media platform called Everyone's Invited; I had a sense that my friends and I were not alone in our experiences. It is a space hosting stories of sexual transgressions of all types, where survivors can share their experiences anonymously. Existing in a system that normalises issues such as slut shaming and sexual bullying can have a traumatic impact on a person, especially when perpetrated over a sustained period. Trauma comes in many forms. It can be repressed, delayed, overt and covert. It manifests in places you would never expect to find it; it creeps up on you, revealing itself in your own behaviours, actions, relationships, friendships and self-worth. The impact of trauma is staggering; it presents in strained intimate relationships, in struggles with vulnerability, trust issues, and panic attacks during sex. Many survivors report long-term problems with their mental health, which can manifest in bouts of depression, increased anxiety, paranoia, hypervigilance, suicidal tendencies, suicide ideation, self-harm and the triggering of eating disorders and body dysmorphia. It is caused by living in a culture that sanctions this behaviour. It changes the way you see yourself and the people around you, it transforms your life experience permanently. It is not something that goes away with time, it is something that you must learn to live with.

· · ·

In June 2020, when I was completing my graduate degree, an incident moved me to share some of my experiences of this culture on Instagram. I had been to a birthday party with friends and whilst I was there someone said something that triggered me: a traumatic experience that I had had a year prior suddenly felt as fresh as the day it happened. I woke up the next morning in a complete state of panic. I was crying uncontrollably, struggling to breathe and unable to speak. Twelve months after it had happened and yet I still found myself being propelled into an emotionally and psychologically debilitating episode. In the aftermath of sexual violence, life can be unbearable and impossible to navigate, where every day is a struggle. I spent a year reeling from that experience, crying almost every day on the bus to university, hyperaware of my surroundings, paranoid, depressed and suicidal. My friendships suffered, I struggled through my essays and seminars, and I lost most of my confidence, purpose and motivation to live my life.

After my panic attack, I called a friend for support and we spoke for two hours on the phone. With every moment, anecdote and experience we shared, we began to understand just how deeply entrenched coercive and abusive behaviour was and how normalised these experiences of violation were. This began to reveal itself further in the many conversations I began having with friends about our time at school and university. Embedded into our daily lives, incidents of harassment didn't feel rare: they were part and parcel of our experience growing up. Whether it was on the Tube, the bus, at home, at school, on the street, at a house party, or in a nightclub – these attacks were happening anywhere and everywhere. The act of a physical assault itself is the tip of the iceberg; the culture of abuse is all around us. It's in the news we read, the films we watch, the music we listen to, the people we surround ourselves with, the institutions we navigate, the laws we follow and the streets we walk. But most importantly, it's within *us*.

When I first shared my story online, I never expected

anything like what happened next. Everyone's Invited wasn't about starting a movement or creating change, it was about sharing my own experience and hoping that other people might relate to it so I might not feel so alone in what I went through. It was about exposing the reality of growing up in this environment and sharing a body of experiences that are so common, yet were so hidden and stigmatised. The act of sharing felt like a release, a moment of catharsis. I remember feeling exposed but I also remember feeling lighter, feeling free.

I was immediately overwhelmed with messages. Old friends, new friends, mutual friends, people I hadn't seen in five years, all reached out to tell me how much their own experiences resonated with mine. As I posted more and more testimonies, people found strength in knowing that they weren't alone. It empowered them to share – and what began as a small moment of sharing for myself spiralled into a chorus of brave voices that would no longer be silenced. When you can relate to something, when you can identify your thoughts, feelings and trauma in someone else's story, you begin to realise something that is simple but also revolutionary: you are not alone.

With this realisation comes the affirmation that you should not be ashamed of what you have been through and that there is community in others who can relate to and understand your trauma. By the end of the first week of sharing these stories on my Instagram, I was overwhelmed and emotionally exhausted. But it will always stay with me as a pivotal moment in my life. There is nothing more powerful than the bonds and profound connections that I built through these deeply personal, intimate conversations, and in the sharing and reading of these stories. Knowing how many of my peers had had these experiences was a heartbreaking revelation, yet it was also deeply moving and uplifting to be empowered by this community.

Sex is generally taboo in most households, as parents and teenagers cringe at the prospect of having real conversations about relationships, sex, consent, sexual violence, rape and image-based abuse. The result is 'turning a blind eye' and choosing to brush it under the carpet, opting to not have the difficult conversations, avoiding the awkwardness and embarrassment of these subjects. At the time, I didn't realise that what seemed so obvious, so 'regular', was actually shocking to the ears of the older generation and that these experiences, our experiences, needed to be articulated to them, with urgency. The act of collecting testimonies and openly hosting them on a website is doing just this: exposing the reality of the modern sexual landscape and by consequence bridging the knowledge gap between the young and the old.

The existence of this gap was only confirmed by some of the older generation's responses to Everyone's Invited. There was widespread shock and, in many cases, a total disbelief and doubt of the validity of these stories. There was a profound unwillingness from some to engage and listen to the lived experiences of the young. Testimonies were often met with a tone of disgust or distaste, and dismissed as 'sordid'. I began to grasp at the time just how limited their understanding is of what it's like to come of age in this modern sexual landscape, and how most parents have next to no idea about what is actually going on in their teenagers' lives.

The testimonies document a spectrum of stories where boundaries are crossed, power is abused and autonomy is stolen. They reveal that teenage girls' earliest and most formative sexual experiences are saturated with shame, embarrassment, humiliation and pain. The experience of dealing with sexual assault as a teen becomes 'the norm of your understanding of what sexual experiences are', said one entry. Sexual harassment, abuse, assault and rape are usually hidden experiences, stigmatised to such an extreme extent that we dare not share them with the people in our lives. The testimonies reveal the many barriers to reporting assault and the deeply complex struggles victims face in the aftermath of sexual violence. When survivors do share, they are often met with disbelief, they are doubted, invalidated, shamed, and ostracised by their peers and communities. Victim-blaming can have a devastating impact on a survivor, on someone who is already fragile and traumatised and just beginning to process their experience. We have been living in a culture that shames victims for their experiences and silences survivors when they come forward to share their stories. Sexual violence shrouds its victims in stigma. Growing up, I don't remember learning much about it in school, or at home. The word 'rape' was taboo, a subject too ugly to discuss openly amongst ourselves and our peers. It felt like something so extreme, unrecognisable, something that happens once in a blue moon, perpetrated by strangers in dark alleyways in the dead of night.

What I realised when I read so many experiences that mirrored my own is that we are all part of a structure that enables this culture – and nobody benefits from it. 'It is a systemic social problem with deep roots in patriarchal belief systems and ideologies about gender, entitlement, power and male dominance,' says activist and author Dr Jackson Katz, and one that we all accept to some degree through centuries and generations of socialisation.[3] It's about the deeply entrenched attitudes that dictate damaging gender stereotypes and norms manifesting in toxic forms of masculinity and femininity. We must recognise that, within this culture, we have been socialised, by default, not only to create such a toxic and harmful environment, but to also sustain it. We are both the victims and the perpetrators.

Dehumanisation is at the heart of this culture and when we strip a person of their humanity they become vulnerable to violation. A teenage boy might think they're simply making an innocent 'joke'. But the misogyny and the sexist attitudes that exist in the social fabric of society feed into the structures that systematically fail survivors. When we allow these behaviours to prevail unchecked we are unknowingly allowing this abuse to continue.

· · ·

When I launched Everyone's Invited, I could never have imagined the impact that it would have. In just one year, my team and I initiated a national conversation with millions of people, received worldwide press coverage, triggered a ground-breaking Ofsted review in schools and necessitated the launch of the NSPCC helpline for abuse in education. We have met with ministers, the Home Office, the Department for Education, the Ministry of Justice, the Department for Transport, the police, and key charities and stakeholders. Everyone's Invited has unleashed a tidal wave of hidden stories – the sheer volume of submissions is a testament to the universal prevalence of sexual violence and the rape culture that we live in.

I'm proud to be working against the stigma and shame that surrounds these issues. Those who have shared their stories with us are incredibly brave. The testimonies themselves are the agents of change; they show us that there is great power in a story. We have learnt that real change is possible, even when it feels unimaginable. To understand, we must be willing to listen, to question our beliefs, our understanding of the world, our own experiences and our belief in what is 'normal'. We will need to let go of the binary and understand humans as complex and intricate beings who are capable of both harm and good. We are all ultimately the products of diverse environments and experiences, we cannot be reduced to a one-dimensional existence. Empathy is needed if we are to open our minds to others' lived experiences and stories.

· · ·

This book is not a memoir; it is not a story in the narrative sense, though it is inspired by the stories of many. When I started writing, I didn't know where I was going; it felt like an insurmountable task. And in many ways it has been. This was, in part, because the subject matter is, and has been, at times, triggering. Although difficult, I wanted to write something that would challenge your point of view. I wanted to write something affirming and cathartic. I wanted to write something that everyone has a stake in, with the lives and the experiences described reflected directly back onto yours.

In these essays, I explore the impact of sexual violence, attempting to understand and trace its origins, through examining the modern sexual landscape. I also consider the complex impact of trauma on an individual's life. I believe that it is transformative and necessary to gain an understanding of how and why harmful behaviour occurs in order to find meaningful solutions to eradicate it. Writing this book has also become a significant component of my own healing journey. I hope these pages might do the same for you.

These essays centre around the experiences of my peers – mainly the experiences of young people; teenagers at school and university students. Yet it is important to clarify that victims of violence and abuse are of all ages and all backgrounds: this can happen to anyone. I alternate between the terms 'victim' and 'survivor' throughout, choosing whichever I feel is most appropriate in the context of the sentence. Both are widely used but many people have their preferred term. Personally, I think that they are important taken together, capturing the evolving journey of an individual in the aftermath of sexual violence.

The more I read and the more I researched, the more I began to understand that whatever I write will only ever be a scratch on the surface. The ideas explored in these essays are merely springboards, my attempt at beginning to investigate enormously challenging and complex topics. My intention is to communicate these ideas and experiences in an engaging but accessible way, to make them as universal as possible.

What I have written is by no means the final word. In this world, there are as many perspectives as there are people.[4] Everyone will experience life in their own way; what may be true for you might not ring true for the next person. I ask you, the reader, to approach this book with empathy and with an open mind – these are real experiences and I have done my best to communicate them in a way that feels authentic, sensitive, and with utmost consideration for those who have bravely shared their most vulnerable moments. I hope this book will open your mind to the possibility of reconciliation, to the importance of empathy, and to the healing power of connection. Together, if we are brave enough to listen and to place ourselves in the shoes of others, we can build a better world where everyone has the right and the opportunity to develop equal, healthy and loving relationships. Where individuals have the freedom and the confidence to live meaningful, full lives free from oppression, violence and abuse.

I also hope this book will inspire you to look inward and then outward. If we want to change this culture we need to push ourselves to introspection, we need to reflect on our own experiences and our own behaviour. It will be a challenge to understand how you may have contributed to this culture – knowingly or unknowingly – and it will be difficult to come to terms with. It's hard to grasp how learnt behaviours, enforced gender stereotypes and norms, and our values may have been deeply harmful to the people in our lives. There may be guilt, there may be shame, and there may be anger and frustration. But these feelings are human ones – they mean that you have the courage to listen, to learn and to empathise with others.

Beyond Gender Scripts

My four-year-old sister is a beautiful child. Every time I see her, I feel a sudden urge to tell her, 'You're so pretty!' I find that I have an unrelenting need to let her know that she's the most beautiful girl in the world. I try not to do this, but others can't seem to help themselves. Strangers have approached my family on the street, in restaurants and in shops to compliment my sister's looks. Since she was two, my father and stepmother have, on numerous occasions, been asked whether they've ever considered 'child modelling' for her. Over the past year, I have noticed my sister beginning to fixate on girly things; she loves wearing dresses and sparkly shoes, she adores her dolls and she wants to be a princess. She reaches out to touch my hair, and exclaims in her tiny little voice, 'Wow it's preeeeetty.' She has, over time, taken more and more of an interest in her appearance, developing an awareness of her looks and the clothes she wears. On her fourth birthday, she received a Barbie doll set, complete with a hot pink car, three outfits, a mini handbag and a tiny iPhone. She was enthralled. On New Year's Eve, I heard a faint tapping sound on my door. Her head emerged, eyes sparkling and with a look of excitement spilling from her smile. 'We have to get ready for the fireworks now!' she squealed. She held her hands behind her back, then pulled them out to reveal an elegant glass bottle of perfume with 'Bonpoint' written in cursive lettering and two small pink cherries on the label. Perched by my side, she began to spray it on her hands and reached over to slather it across my face.

'What are you doing?' I asked.

'I'm putting perfume on you,' she explained. 'You need perfume if you want to look like a princess.' She leant forward, balancing on one foot as she stretched her arm to apply the scent to the middle of my forehead and down to the tip of my nose.

'Why are you putting it on my nose?' I was laughing by now. She giggled and smiled, reaching towards me again.

'Even on your chinny chin chin!'

'But why do we need to look like princesses?' I enquired.

She stopped for a moment, put her hands on her hips and defiantly declared, 'Because otherwise people will think we are not pretty and we need to be pretty for the fireworks.' She continued to move her fingers lightly with consideration and care, adding the final touches as she warned, 'Make sure it doesn't go in your eyes. Put a little bit here and a little bit here. There. You look pretty now. You look like a princess.'

After birth, a baby is sorted into one of two groups: male or female. Sex is widely seen as a biological determinant. Sex will determine how this human will be viewed, treated and received in society. Gender socialisation begins almost immediately after the baby is categorised, shaping and developing the beginnings of identity from a very early age. The World Health Organization defines gender as referring

> to the characteristics of women, men, girls and boys that are socially constructed. This includes norms, behaviours and roles associated with being a woman, man, girl or boy, as well as relationships with each other. As a social construct, gender varies from society to society and can change over time.[1]

Whilst sex is widely considered biological, gender is constructed by culture and imposed at birth. The social constructionist theory guides this understanding and conceptualisation of gender development in its situation of gender as a social creation[2] and not as a naturally existing category. This will inevitably hold consequences for how people navigate within this environment.[3] What are the implications of sex and gender? Male or female, masculine or feminine, blue or pink, trousers or dresses, trucks or dolls, breadwinner or housewife, mother or father, dominant or submissive, confident or shy, hard or soft. The influence of these gendered roles and stereotypes deeply permeates our lives and daily experiences. Behavioural patterns and decisions such as career paths, clothing choices, parental roles, romantic relationships, personal and professional inter-actions, are all profoundly influenced and shaped by perceptions of gender. The social purpose of the body is decided by these early divisions. What is the purpose of said body? Who are the leaders and who follows? Who wields power and who is subordinate? Who provides and who depends? How does culture define and determine how these bodies interact? How are they controlled and defined by gender scripts?

In consideration of scripts, what springs to mind imme-diately is the idea of performance. Scripts are an external imposition of prewritten ideas, narratives or rules. The result is an inauthentic presentation of self, drawn not from within, but determined and controlled by exterior forces. The American Psychological Association defines a gender script as a temporally organised, gender-related sequence of events.[4] The word *organised* feels definitive, as if such a script has been preordained or predetermined and is grounded in history, suggesting that these early divisions date back centuries. *Sequence of events* is a notable choice of phrase. It implies that early divisions are like pebbles tossed to water, eliciting an infinite rippling, setting into motion a shaping and defining and determining that will profoundly influence the trajectory of the baby's life. The APA's defi-nition also includes examples of stereotypical male and female activities, such as 'building a birdhouse or barbecuing' for men and 'doing laundry or preparing dinner in the kitchen' for women. These stereotypes invite a feeling of absurdity; they are too simplistic and so far from the reality of the modern world. Yet, since the start of the pandemic, women in the US have left the labour force at twice the rate of men, with female paid labour force participation being now at its lowest in more than thirty years.[5] With school closures and kids forced to stay home, women have largely taken on the responsibility of childcare, home schooling and housework. But this trend is apparently nothing new, as this decline in women's roles outside the home has been growing steadily since the financial crisis of 2008, with the pandemic itself just accelerating an already existing problem. Women, pandemics aside, are 43 per cent more likely to leave their jobs once they have children to become stay-at-home mums who bear the brunt of responsibility for childcare in the early years of their children's adolescence.[6] This is the implication of the female script of motherhood: that she must perform not only the birthing, but also the nurturing and the caring for her children.

Gender scripts are analysed throughout this book through the lens of masculinity and femininity; social constructs that impose a script of stereotypical qualities traditionally associated with men and women. Male traits include qualities such as strength, dominance, independence and self-reliance, whilst female traits include compassion, empathy, love, dependence and nurture. These traits taken alone are not unhealthy or harmful, but they become problematic when they are not shared equally between men and women;

instead, they are strictly divided and enforced across gender lines. When these scripts are oppressively imposed, human beings become restricted. This is noted by contemporary writer Olivia Laing, who points to the 1948 Universal Declaration of Human Rights, which 'safeguards the right to a nation and the right to be safe from imprisonment, but not the right to express one's own personal experience of gender; nor to choose, within the absolute limits of consent, with whom and how one wishes to conduct a sexual life'.[7] This is poignant because

> a body can be a prison too. You can exile or incarcerate someone simply by defining them against their own living sense of who they are, by forbidding them love or erotic range. And then, of course, you can make their life a misery, regulate their clothes, their use of lavatories and changing rooms, stop them being able to work or marry.[8]

The gender scripts that we abide by as determined by the bodies we inhabit have the propensity to incarcerate, to restrict, and consequently destroy our authentic selves. The self, the human self, one's sense of identity, the very nature of humanity, as defined by its infinite state of flux, rails against restriction and towards the freedom of expression.

Radical, both of his time and our time, is the work of Magnus Hirschfeld, German physician, sexologist and outspoken advocate of sexual minorities in the early twentieth century. At the heart of his work was a profound exploration of the diversity of gender and sexuality. Hirschfeld was born to Jewish parents on the Baltic coast in a Prussian town. Here, he started studying first modern languages and then, later, medicine. In this time, he gained a doctoral degree and began a practice in Magdeburg in 1894. Once he moved to Berlin, he started his scientific studies in sexuality, research that he felt would ultimately encourage a tolerance of sexual minorities in society. His research in sexology was grounded in activism and empiricism as well as a conviction that the sexual ideology of Judeo-Christian civilisation presented a significant obstacle to the understanding of sexuality. In 1897, Hirschfeld was a part of the world's very first gay rights organisation, the Scientific-Humanitarian Committee; in 1899, he started the *Yearbook of Intermediate Sexual Types* (the first journal dealing with sexual variants); in 1910, he published a study on cross-dressing, *The Transvestites*; and in 1919, he opened the Institute of Sexual Science in Berlin, which was the first sexology institute in the world. In 1910, Hirschfeld calculated forty-three million possible combinations of gender and sexuality after interviewing thousands of people whose variety of physical appearance, sexual desire and genitalia amazed him. 'The number of actual and imaginable sexual varieties is almost unending,' he claimed. 'In each person there is a different mixture of manly and womanly substances, and as we cannot find two leaves alike on a tree, then it is highly unlikely that we will find two humans whose manly and womanly characteristics exactly match in kind and number.'[9] Although radical in his thinking, Hirschfeld's findings lean towards tolerance of a multiplicity of gender expression and variety, challenging a binary conception of gender identity and sexuality.

Throughout history, similar ideas can be traced about the various combinations of male and female traits and characteristics. Despite the mainstream Victorian view that masculinity and femininity were inborn and sexuality was immutable, sexologists, writers and artists of this time period nevertheless championed the fluidity and the artifice of gender. Virginia Woolf's 1928 novel *Orlando*, for example, is a story concerned with challenging fixed notions of gender and identity. 'In every human being a vacillation from one sex to the other takes place, and often it is only the clothes that keep the male or female likeness, while underneath the sex is the very opposite of what it is above.' In her extended essay *A Room of One's Own*, Woolf once again returns to this idea of vacillation between sexes in the taxi cab analogy she presents at the book's conclusion: 'When I saw the couple get into the taxi cab the mind felt as if, after being divided, it had come together again in a natural fusion.' Woolf's androgynous vision, in this fluid combination of masculinity and femininity, implies, once again, that both masculine and feminine characteristics are needed for a kind of ideal or hybrid form of humanity, where one can achieve 'complete satisfaction and happiness' in the unification of sexes. In the 1890s, a contemporary of Woolf's, philosopher, early activist for gay rights and open homosexual Edward Carpenter, contended the existence of a 'third' or 'intermediate sex', which he named the 'urnings' (from the goddess Urania, meaning heaven), a term originally coined by Karl Heinrich Ulrichs.[10] For Carpenter, 'urnings' are divine in their capacity to achieve an 'androgynous transcendence' of a narrow, restrictive form of heterosexuality.[11] These androgynous ideals can also be seen in T. S. Eliot's poem *The Waste Land* (1922). Eliot envisions the iconic hermaphrodite figure Tiresias: 'I Tiresias though blind, throbbing between two lives, / Old man with wrinkled female breasts'.[12] In this being there is an essential sense of androgyny needed to make up the all-knowing universal observer. Tiresias is a figure from Greek mythology, a blind Theban seer who is the son of the nymph Chariclo, a favourite of the goddess Athena. He is famous for living as a man, then a woman, and then a man once again. Tiresias, despite his blindness, was endowed with the gifts of prophetic vision and long life.

Woolf, Hirschfeld, Carpenter and Eliot champion the fluidity of identity and self. They resist the forces that seek to stagnate and oppressively define complex beings who are always growing, moving and evolving. Gender scripts – when strictly enforced by societal pressures – are confining. Could moving away from the categories and the binaries and moving closer towards both an acceptance and understanding of gender role fluidity – as suggested by these thinkers – be an optimum way of being, which will allow humans to reach their highest potential? An individual who is free to embrace both masculinity and femininity, who is free to enjoy the traits and characteristics traditionally associated with both, who can exercise traditional 'male' strength, leadership, and empowerment as well as the 'female' compassion, kindness and emotional sensitivity is one who can live a fulfilling and rewarding life. If men and women were to embrace fluidity in gender roles what would the world look like? Would more women, in embracing the 'male' trait of confidence, assume more political positions of power and, in turn, prioritise advocating against abuse and harassment in society, because women (the largest group affected) have endured the burden of sexual trauma throughout historical time? Would more men, if they embraced traditional 'female' empathy, challenge abusive and predatory behaviour, hold their friends accountable and become well-informed role models for positive change?

Boys and girls, men and women, and everyone in between must have *emotional literacy* in the depths of depression, they need *courage* to leave an abusive relationship, *confidence* to achieve their goals in life, they require *compassion* to help those in need, and should be able to embrace *empathy* to forgive those who have wronged them. In the essays that follow, by exploring the damaging impact of the enforcement of gender scripts, I have endeavoured to champion the importance of striving for this balance. I hope to encourage you to resist the incarceration of self, to embrace 'male' and 'female' traits, qualities and characteristics and be unafraid to occupy liminal spaces. Dance along the spectrum as you please, traversing the lines of traditional gender scripts.

There is nothing wrong with dresses, skirts, baby dolls, ballet shoes and kitchen sets. And, equally, there is nothing wrong with toy cars, planes, trucks, footballs and action figures. The issues arise when we don't get opportunities as young children to play with both. I want my baby sister to learn about the importance of consideration for others as she does when she cradles her baby doll. But I also want her to feel freedom and believe that anything is possible whilst sprinting down a football pitch and scoring a goal. I want her to save the world and be an unstoppable force for good like an action figure of a fearless superhero. Why can't she develop her creativity and skills in ballet class but also learn more practical skills through learning how planes fly or cars drive? When we enforce just the former or the latter, we are, whether we're aware of it or not, imbuing in our children a pervasive gender socialisation. Because these toys are more than just objects, they are messages, they are the beginnings of ideology.

Pain is Normal

In April 2021, in response to the testimonies published on the Everyone's Invited website, Ofsted was asked by the government to commission a rapid review of sexual abuse in schools and colleges. The findings of this review confirmed the work of Everyone's Invited in its conclusion that sexual harassment and sexual abuse online had become both normalised and pervasive across all schools in the UK. The day before the report was published, I went to film an interview in Victoria Tower Gardens with Sky News. This was my first interview of the day, with four more to follow and thirteen back-to-back interviews to complete on the day of publication. Nervous, conscious of the national platform I'd been given and the immense pressure to perform, I arrived early, sweating in my summer suit, under the heat of a harsh sun and a blinding blue sky. The reporter who greeted me was friendly, he praised my 'important' work and asked me questions about Everyone's Invited. He told me about how his children, who went to schools in London, were also deeply engaged with our work. The cameraman had positioned me in the middle of the park so that I was directly facing the bright sun. I was blinded by sunshine and, distracted by this, I struggled to recall my key messages. I didn't want to risk making a mistake on national television, so I politely asked the cameraman if there was any way we could move to a shady patch, just a few steps from where we were standing. His response was stubborn; he insisted that I 'looked better' in the sun, asserting that he knew what was best for the shot, but I stood my ground. The cameraman rolled his eyes as he packed up his equipment to move a few metres to the left. I found myself apologising profusely, an almost instinctive reaction, suddenly feeling guilty for asserting my right to be able to see whilst answering questions about sexual violence on national television in front of millions of people. After we finished the interview, the reporter turned to the cameraman. Mockingly, he asked, 'Why don't we move over? The sun's in my eyes.' He smirked, rolled his eyes and they both proceeded to laugh in my face. It felt like the two men, twice my age, were relishing the feeling of making a nervous twenty-two-year-old feel stupid and small. I was immediately transported back to my teenage years, over-whelmed with the familiar feeling of insignificance and humiliation I felt when I was bullied by teenage boys on group chats and laughed at for speaking my mind or asserting an opinion.

Of course, I should have said something at the time,

but the men should not have treated me in that way. The irony of this moment is laughable. When they left, I kicked myself. *What's wrong with you?* I scolded. *Why didn't I say something? What the hell am I doing in this campaign if I can't stand up for myself in real life? Why did I immediately apologise? Why did I instinctively seek to diffuse tension and avoid confrontation at all costs?* We need to ask questions about the way women and girls are socialised to be polite, reserved and diffuse tension in their daily lives. Why do women passively respond to and accept humiliation, discomfort and pain?

. . .

Femininity is about conforming to a set of rules that are stereotypically associated with women in society. A socially constructed set of expectations, attributes and roles that dictate how women should behave, speak and carry themselves in life. The *Oxford English Dictionary* defines femininity as the 'Behaviour or qualities regarded as characteristic of a woman; feminine quality or characteristics; womanliness'. Typical traits associated with women include gentleness, empathy, humility, receptivity and sensitivity. These traits by themselves are positive, they are commendable, important values that all human beings should strive towards. However, too much emphasis on conforming to this narrow script can become harmful for both women and the people in their lives. Subscribing to the social script of femininity is about maintaining a performance, adhering to the socially encoded stereotypical roles of wife, mother, daughter or host. The implications of unrelenting gender performances are explored in Zadie Smith's novel *NW*. Natalie is a successful Black middle-class lawyer, wife and mother who is the picture of meritocratic achievement, skyrocketing from her council flat to middle-class lawyerly success. But we learn that her constant performance of roles enforced on her by the world and society she inhabits leaves only, in the end, a gaping emptiness.

> Daughter drag. Sister drag. Mother drag. Wife drag. Court drag. Rich drag. Poor drag. British drag. Jamaican drag. Each required a different wardrobe. But when considering these various attitudes she struggled to think what would be the most authentic, or perhaps the least inauthentic.[1]

Natalie's life is defined and dictated by performance after performance. Society's incessant drumbeat of roles associated with femininity creates a sense of duty in Natalie that she feels obligated to fulfil, to the extent where she has, over time, grounded the very kernel of her existence in the daily execution of such roles. In the end, her life is dictated not by her own free will, but by the needs of others and by the expectations enforced on her by her family, community and society. Engineered for the consumption of others, these drag personae eventually consume her and, by the end of the novel, reveal only an absence of self when the curtains are finally drawn. Katie Anthony, freelance journalist, suggests women are locked into a performance that restricts them as humans, where they have been taught to live for others, constantly subordinating their own needs by putting the desires and comfortability of others before their own.[2] Shame is a powerful force that keeps these gender scripts in check. Psychologist Helen Block Lewis identified a link between shame, gender and an individual's subjective process of identity construction. According to Lewis, women and girls are prone to shame in two significant ways, the first being how they are socialised from an early age to define themselves not by independence or individual autonomy, but primarily in terms of their relationships and dependence on others. Secondly, girls are particularly vulnerable to social pressures due to this defining sense of interdependence, especially those that encourage them to adhere to traditional concepts and rules of femininity. A vision of femininity that is, at heart, socially defined encourages in women and girls an internalisation of anxiety and anger, 'turning against the self', as any open expression of hostility and anger is discouraged. They are marked then by feelings of blame and self-censure during these moments of threat, discomfort or frustration.[3] Affirming these ideas is psychologist Michael Lewis, who also saw a 'strong correlation between women and a propensity to organize evaluative information about the self around feelings of shame.'[4] In his study on gender shame, Lewis found amongst college students poignant marked gender differences between what triggered feelings of shame in men versus what triggered the same feelings in women. Men, on the one hand, identified two areas that triggered feelings of shame: failure related to sexual potency, and failure in a job-related task or performance in sport. On the other hand, shame elicited in women was the most prevalent in two circumstances: the first being physical attractiveness, and the second and most significant was the failure to maintain interpersonal relationships. Such differences on account of gender will arise, as noted by Lewis, from gender role socialisation.[5]

Throughout my teenage years and early adulthood, I felt an inexorable pressure to be in a relationship and that this was somehow one of the most important pursuits of my being – that I would not be fulfilled or 'whole' without a boy or a man with whom I would ground my identity; someone who would 'complete me'. Do you have a boyfriend yet? Is there a boy in your life? Who are you dating? These are the questions that single girls and women are repeatedly bombarded with. I have genuinely felt a consistent overwhelming sense of shame and failure in being single as I have internalised the message that a woman's capacity to be with a man is the most important measure of her worth. Female worth is defined by our relationships, dependence on others, physical attractiveness, the way we look and carry ourselves, how society receives us and perceives us, male attention, and the validation of our peers. For centuries, women and girls have been encouraged to ignore their own psychological and physical needs to sustain the needs of those around them. Instead of defining who we are and finding value from within, we look outward, to society, to both define and determine us. When we live in this way, we restrict ourselves, we are oppressed by the confines of the 'feminine' script. There is too much emphasis on adhering to a narrow script that limits us and stops us from being whole, from being fully human. Instead, women have been taught to exist for the pleasure of others. Katie Anthony raised the question of whether toxic femininity exists. '"Toxic femininity" (if it exists),' she wrote, 'encourages silent acceptance of violence and domination in order to survive . . . It's a thing women do to keep our value, which the patriarchy has told us is conditional upon our ability to bear violent domination.'[6]

There is a sense of being trapped in a performance, visible in the ways in which we respond, repress and ignore any pain or discomfort that we might experience. 'Centuries of conditioning by society and the media have encultured women to be uncomfortable most of the time and to ignore this discomfort.'[7] Our beauty rituals exemplify our tolerance for discomfort and pain; the plucking, shaving, waxing, needles, surgeries, straightening, curling and the heels we wear. Most men don't need to get their hair waxed off their genitals or undergo life-threatening surgeries to be perceived as sexually 'viable' or conventionally attractive by social media's beauty standards.[8] American feminist activist and writer Andrea Dworkin argued in *Woman Hating: A Radical Look at Sexuality* (1974) that pain is a fundamental element of the grooming practice for women. A woman's effort to maintain her femininity and desirability through painful beauty rituals cultivates a deep conditioning in girls, an acceptance that pain is an inevitable part of their existence. Dworkin wrote that, 'The pain, of course, teaches an important lesson: no price is too great, no process too repulsive, no operation too painful for the woman who would be beautiful.' Steeped into our culture is a shared and silent understanding that beauty is pain, an idea so deeply embedded and so normalised that we barely notice it.[9] It is alive in the media, in the films we watch and is passed down through lessons we learn from our mothers. It was supermodel Kate Moss who famously summed it up: 'Nothing tastes as good as skinny feels.' We accept pain and discomfort as normal, as part and parcel of womanhood.

A theme that runs through many of the testimonies on Everyone's Invited is the tolerance of uncomfortable or painful experiences. It would not be an exaggeration to say that every girl and woman I know has had some form of traumatic experience on the spectrum of harassment, coercion and rape that has left them with a lingering feeling of violation and trauma. The testimonies reveal how violation often warrants a passive response from victims. Many report a 'ritualised' form of sexual harassment on school premises. As students are groped in school corridors, slut shamed, or humiliated by crude comments and derogatory remarks, they learn to 'laugh it off' and dismiss these experiences as 'no big deal', and in doing so ensure that they are still 'liked', 'popular', 'fun'. They are 'cool girls' who can take a joke. Cool enough to be considered 'one of the guys'. Yet, we have learnt from the testimonies that these smaller sexual transgressions do have a profound impact on self-confidence, mental health and self-worth, especially when they are repeatedly perpetrated during such formative years.

Many of the testimonies report a much darker and disturbing manifestation of this tolerance for discomfort. Young girls describe submissively adhering to coercion, to an unspoken expectation that they 'owe' a boy some sexual pleasure if they were to begin a sexual encounter with them. Or even when they just find themselves alone with a boy in a setting that could be perceived as intimate, as was common in the scenario of a girl going back to a boy's house to 'hang out' and then suddenly being confronted with the expectation of sex. Many describe the expectation that boys have, and the anger, violence or humiliation girls sometimes face when they refuse to submit to the pressure of performing sex acts. Growing up, giving a boy a blow job was nothing unusual. It was an almost casual exchange, totally normalised amongst my peers as something girls did at house parties in the bathroom or garden behind the bushes. As suggested by Peggy Orenstein in *Girls & Sex*, 'giving head' was a way for many girls to adhere to the obligatory expectation of pleasure with the minimum potential for physical, social or emotional bother. Girls often opted to give blow jobs to boys to avoid having sex, which was considered a 'bigger deal' with more stigma and social repercussions amongst our peers. Orenstein uncovered in her interviews a pervasive and inherent priority to please trumped the pursuit of actual sexual pleasure, and was somehow entrenched in our understanding of sex and sexual relationships. Girls were acutely self-conscious in these intimate moments, more concerned about their performance, how they looked, and how much pleasure they were giving rather than actually engaging in and attempting to feel any pleasure in sex.[10] This rings true to what I read in some of the testimonies as well as the experiences of my peers. Just as Orenstein reported in her interviews, many testimonies from Everyone's Invited repeatedly report the same experience of teenage boys coercing girls into giving them oral sex. This was either done verbally, online with a barrage of manipulative messages, or by physical coercion in the spur of the moment with the infamous 'head push' or 'shoulder push' – where a boy would forcibly push a girl's head towards his groin. The girls reported acute feelings of degradation, humiliation and violation, with some sharing that the experience scarred them for years, creating a complete aversion to sex in any form, even within trusted, consensual relationships. April Burns, an assistant professor of psychology at City University of New York, in her research on high school girls and oral sex found that girls, in this day and age, saw fellatio like a 'form of homework' or a 'chore to be done', 'a skill to master' and that, as with schoolwork, they were worried about their performance. Although they did report a feeling of satisfaction in completing the task successfully, the form of pleasure described was not physical. The research concluded that they had become socialised as 'learners' rather than 'yearners'.[11] Another common theme that cropped up again and again in the testimonies was the teenage boys' manipulation of the term 'blue balls' as a sinister strategy to coerce girls into unwanted sexual acts. 'If we stop, you'll give me blue balls' and 'You have to give me head now or you'll give me blue balls'. The phrase itself is a colloquial term to describe the discomfort experienced when sexual activity is stopped before the point of orgasm as a result of increased blood flow, a sensation that can be felt by both sexes, yet girls are socialised to cope with sexual discomfort whilst boys are socialised to expect sexual satisfaction.

In the eyes of some men and boys, the very act of sex is seen as an act of ownership, as if consenting to vaginal sex gives them automatic entitlement to do whatever they want. The rising tolerance of discomfort in girls taken to its extreme is seen repeatedly throughout the testimonies in descriptions of graphic instances of non-consensual slapping, choking and anal penetration midway through consensual sex. Anal sex, in recent years, has been on the rise amongst teenagers due to its increased prevalence in pornography. A study conducted in 2014 of heterosexuals aged between sixteen and twenty-eight found boys were most likely to push for 'fifth base', approaching it as a competition amongst other boys rather than a form of intimacy between themselves and their partner. The boys made the assumption that girls would need to be and could be coerced into the act, whilst girls were expected to endure it despite the consistent reporting of pain.[12] Deborah Tolman, psychologist and co-founder of the movement SPARK (Sexualization Protest: Action, Resistance, Knowledge), has deemed anal sex as the 'new oral', claiming, 'Since all girls are now presumed to have oral sex in their repertoire, anal sex is becoming the new "Will she do it or not?" behavior, the new "Prove you love me".' She goes on to say that female sexual pleasure is still not considered or prioritised.[13] American research scientist and sex educator Debby Herbenick said that it is, 'A metaphor, a symbol in one concrete behavior for the lack of education about sex, the normalization of female pain, and the way what had once been stigmatized has, over the course of a decade, become expected. If you don't want to do it, you're suddenly not good enough, you're frigid, you're missing out, you're not exploring your sexuality, you're not adventurous.'[14]

A passive response perpetuates a harmful cycle of acceptance resulting in the normalisation of damaging behaviour. Peer-on-peer normalisation of abusive behaviour is powerful and oppressive, as those who challenge it are ridiculed, gaslighted or humiliated by their friends. The continual institutional failure of schools to adequately respond to allegations and reports of harmful sexual behaviour reinforces this status quo, doubling down on the message that discomfort and pain are inevitable experiences of life for young girls.

As a teenager, these messages of expecting and accepting pain were passed down to the younger years by the older girls at my single-sex boarding school, as they are in schools across the country. From the age of thirteen, we were allocated boarding houses where we shared big dorms with older girls from different years. Some students enforced a tradition that meant that in the first week of the September term, after lights out, older girls in the dorm would 'corrupt' the youngest girls. We huddled together, with a single torch, and whispered under our bed sheets; 'corruption' was a scandalous and silly affair. The older girls saturated our young, impressionable minds with skewed, funny, and problematic ideas of sex and relationships, passed down through the years by the generations of older pupils. Intimate and graphic details about everything from flirting, the 'bases', touching, fingering, oral sex, vaginal sex and anal sex were audaciously dissected in dramatic monologues. One of the first things I learnt about sex from my fellow students was that the experience of 'losing my virginity' was going to be a painful one. 'Don't be scared, everyone has to do it,' I was informed. 'You just have to grit your teeth and get it over and done with,' reassured another. 'You might cry, but don't let them see.' And, 'It's only humiliating if you bleed all over the sheets.' I was advised to have a drink beforehand to make the whole ordeal easier. The message was crystal clear: sex was an inevitably painful ritual that all teenage girls would go through. Media critic Lili Loofbourow writes on this initiation to sex and how it impacts our understanding and perception of sex, which can be carried through into intimate relationships throughout our lifetime. 'Think about how that initiation into sex might thwart your ability to recognize "discomfort" as something that's *not* supposed to happen. When sex keeps hurting long after virginity is lost, as it did for many of my friends, many a woman assumes *she's* the one with the problem. And, well, if you were supposed to grit your teeth and get through it the first time, why not the second? At what point does sex magically transform from *enduring* someone doing something to you that you don't like?'[15]

Research conducted in the US by the National Library of Medicine shows that 30 per cent of women and 5 per cent of men report pain during their most recent sexual event. Furthermore, 72 per cent report pain during anal sex and 'large proportions' don't tell their partner when sex hurts. The research concludes that pain is a relatively common and often not discussed aspect of both vaginal and anal intercourse between women and men.[16] Many of the testimonies submitted to Everyone's Invited detail how many teenagers and women experience extreme discomfort or pain during sex and relationships. Psychotherapist and sex educator Kim Loliya has stated that, 'Women can feel like they can't speak up when they're in pain during sex; it's the societal indoctrination that says "girls should be seen and not heard". When pain arises, women often think there's something wrong with them, and fear how that will impact their partner. They feel responsible for the pain, and embarrassed by it. Often, women completely miss that their pain is triggered by their body feeling unsafe.'[17] Researcher Sara McClelland conducted a study in the US that asked men and women to describe what low sexual satisfaction meant to them. Men reported experiences of 'boredom' and unresponsive partners, whereas the women frequently answered 'pain'.[18] Loofbourow delves deeper into the idea of 'bad sex', exploring a disturbing discrepancy between the male and female experiences. She writes: 'I've been dumbstruck by the flattening work of that phrase – specifically, the assumption that "bad sex" means the same thing to men who have sex with women as it does to women who have sex with men.'[19] She goes on to quote from McClelland: 'While women imagined the low end to include the potential for extremely negative feelings and the potential for pain, men imagined the low end to represent the potential for less satisfying sexual outcomes, but they never imagined harmful or damaging outcomes for themselves.'[20] Debby Herbenick sums up this disparity of female and male expectations: 'When it comes to "good sex", women often mean without pain, men often mean they had orgasms.'[21]

Sexual pleasure was never spoken about in my Personal, Social, Health and Citizenship Education (PSHCE) lessons at school. Not once is sexual pleasure mentioned in the Relationships and Sex Education statutory guidance. When I reflect upon my teenage years, I can't help but feel a deep sadness for the way I was taught about what to expect from sex and relationships. As a young, vulnerable and impressionable girl, I should have been given the tools, knowledge and confidence to cultivate my own sexual agency and pleasure. Why was pain in sex normalised by other girls?

42

Why was it framed as not only an expectation but an inevitability? Why didn't anyone teach me otherwise? It's crucial that young girls are taught that their sexual pleasure matters too. Women are not passive recipients, they should have the confidence to explore sex, discover what they enjoy and engage in pleasurable, meaningful, loving relationships with intimate partners. When the subject of sexual pleasure is taboo in the classroom and taboo at home, young people grow up with an absence of understanding about the importance of mutual pleasure in intimate relationships. Girls need to be taught that their desire, sexual pleasure and agency matter too.

In the TV series *Fleabag*, Phoebe Waller-Bridge penned the famous 'menopause' speech, which opens as follows: 'Women are born with pain built in. It is our physical destiny; period pains, sore boobs, childbirth, you know. We carry it within ourselves throughout our lives.' For women, pain is everywhere. It's in the body. It's engendered through centuries of social conditioning. It's in painful beauty practices, in the tolerance of pain in sex, in the prioritising of the comfortability of others before our own – whatever the cost. This has somehow coerced in us a passive acceptance and tolerance of sexual harassment, verbal abuse, coercion and violence. Many women have not stood up for themselves, they haven't called it out, and they have stayed silent because centuries of conditioning and cultural indoctrination have imbued in us a pervasive understanding that pain is inevitable. That pain is the default. That pain is normal.

The Cost of Beauty

Back in August 2020, I was approached by a journalist from a national paper after sharing on my Instagram the initial surge of stories that I received detailing my peers' experiences of misogyny, sexual harassment, image-based abuse, sexual assault and rape. After conducting the interview, the journalist asked to use my image to run with the story. At the time, I didn't feel ready to do this; to lose my anonymity, to have my image used and reused and taken from me, a relinquishing of autonomy and identity to the public sphere. I firmly refused this request yet she asked again and again, insisting that the story's lifespan and mobility would be increased. In the end, the story never ran; I suspected, at the time, that my choice to retain my image played a key role in the final editorial decision. Months later, in March 2021, I would be approached by another journalist from a national paper who also asked for the use of my image to run with my interview. With a stronger foundation of support and a group of volunteers, I felt more ready to lead a public campaign and I agreed, hoping the decision would help amplify the voices of survivors with maximum impact. The story ran as the lead Saturday interview, a double-page spread in the paper and, most shockingly, my image, taken on a sunny day in a park in the north of Paris, was enormous and plastered across the front page. A media storm was ignited that would go on not for weeks, but for almost four months. In thousands of articles and hundreds of interviews, Everyone's Invited was covered extensively by every paper and news outlet in the country and by hundreds of international press outlets from around the world. A few months later, when I was back in London, I met up with a journalist for a coffee. 'You know, Soma, in the end, they only put you on the front page because of the way you look.'

Culturally, female success in life is still, to this day, deeply rooted in a woman's ability to appear beautiful, to be admired and to be seen, if at all. In many ways, life is immeasurably easier if you are considered a beautiful woman. The roots of these messages are deeply implicit in every aspect of life. From getting higher marks at school for handing in the same quality of work, to being treated more favourably as a 'cute' kid, to advancing more quickly in your career, to obtaining a higher salary, to having your pick of the dating pool, and to being less likely judged as 'guilty' in a courtroom.[1] Attractive women are statistically more likely to be hired over 'unattractive' women according to the study 'Searching for a job is a beauty contest' by the University of Messina. The research found that 'unattractive' women had only a 7 per cent call-back rate, whilst 'attractive' women were called back 54 per cent of the time.

Pretty women, beautiful women, attractive women, women who adhere to Eurocentric and Western society's beauty standards do in many ways enjoy an enormous advantage in life. Take for example the women who are worshipped in Western media: the actresses, models and influencers who are endlessly praised and rewarded for their display of unobtainable beauty. They preside over the rest of us like divine figures, the winners who take all the opportunities, the career advancements, the magazine covers, the sponsorships, the invites to the most exclusive events, the endless stream of free stuff and, of course, the status and the clout. From celebrity brand deals to partnerships, the capitalisation of beauty and status is nothing new; celebrities and influencers have built empires off their image and ability to captivate the audience of millions. Building a commercial business often comes hand in hand with attaining celebrity or influencer status.

Celebrities, influencers and TikTokers are the ruling class of the virtual world. Positioned at the apex of societal beauty standards, they capitalise on their image and continue to uphold the impossible beauty standards that wield such pervasive power and influence over young and impressionable minds. Image is commodified online. Brand deals promoting fit teas, waist trainers and beauty products come with six- and eight-figure payments, which are bestowed onto users with anywhere from tens of thousands to millions of followers. As the most followed person on Instagram, footballer Cristiano Ronaldo shot to the top of Instagram's rich list, making as much as $1.6 million from a single sponsored post. He is estimated to be making more than $40 million annually from Instagram alone. Following closely behind is actor Dwayne Johnson who can charge $1.52 million per post, then Ariana Grande at $1.51 million and Kylie Jenner who can command $1.49 million. Social media now drives a $500 billion global beauty industry, targeting Gen Z as one of its most crucial demographics. In 2020, the global weight management market was estimated at more than $260 billion and is now projected to grow to more than $400 billion by 2027.

But what are the implications of striving towards, obtaining and maintaining impossible beauty standards? What does it really mean to be beautiful? And what is, in the end, the cost of beauty?

• • •

Just like my younger sister, I, too, as a child, was repeatedly told by teachers in the classroom, by my extended family and by older girls at my drama club that I was 'cute' and 'pretty'. This overemphasis on how I looked taught me to prioritise my appearance above all things. Whilst my older sister was the 'smart' one and the 'cool girl' who derived her confidence and self-worth from her studies, skills and intellectual abilities, I was the 'cute' and 'pretty' sister who internalised, over time, the message that my worth in this world was measured by my capacity to be admired, to look beautiful. Having learnt this 'message' early, throughout my teenage years I became obsessed with other people's perception of my appearance and the validation I gained from adhering to the beauty standards that were held amongst my peers.

It was at the intersection of beauty standards and social media where things really began to take an enormous toll on my mental and physical health. Growing up, joining social media and creating accounts on Facebook, Instagram and Tumblr began to exacerbate my fixation on my image and the way it was perceived by others. From the age of thirteen, I used to scroll on Tumblr for hours at a time, poring over images of slender supermodels with immaculate bodies, flawless skin and sizable thigh gaps. Cara Delevingne, Karlie Kloss and the rest of the Victoria's Secret 'Angels' dominated the beauty standards of the 2010s. Stick thin, long legs, blonde luscious locks, thigh gaps and glistening spotless faces were positioned as the ultimate and unobtainable vision of Western beauty. These bodies and faces did not resemble my twelve- to fourteen-year-old self; a half Chinese, short and curvy girl with thick thighs, hormonal acne and braces. My non-thigh-gap legs were one of my biggest insecurities as a young teenager; they felt ugly, as did stretch marks, rounder faces and hairy armpits. No young girl should be made to feel this way about their body, especially in these early years of development.

In my final years of school, food, eating, weight and body

image completely took over my life. Hours of my days were consumed by planning my meals, thinking about food, restricting my food intake and overexercising to lose weight. By the end of each day I could recount every item of food I'd consumed and calculate my exact calorie intake. For over two years, I spent hours poring over diet plans and researching food and weight loss regimes. I saw food in a binary way; low calorie foods were 'healthy' and high calorie sugary foods weren't. There was a period at boarding school where my daily diet consisted of half of a small packet of Alpen cereal with half an apple for breakfast and only vegetables for lunch and dinner. No carbs would ever be included in any of my meals. I'd obsessively monitor my weight by stepping on scales every morning. I found myself in a toxic cycle of eating, which would go as follows: restrict, starve, exercise then binge. Bingeing would propel me into a depression, I would punish myself and start all over again. Living this way was exhausting; food and eating consumed me both physically and psychologically. Not only did I lose an unhealthy amount of weight in a short space of time to the point where I resembled a coat hanger more than a teenage girl, I also lost my personality, my drive and sense of self in an incessant compulsion to live up to an impossible beauty standard. In the pursuit of the validation of others, I tortured myself in the name of 'beauty'.

I still, to this day, have a chronic fear of wearing shorts, which is, of course, completely absurd. Impossible beauty standards now exist most evidently in the realms of TikTok and Instagram, 'slim thick' is the new standard in the age of Kardashian — a never-ending scroll of perfect bodies, flawless skin, peach bums and tiny waists. Writing in the *New York Times*, journalist Lindsay Crouse highlights how social media only accelerates an age-old cultural lesson: the way in which girls are taught to prioritise the way they are admired by others.

> For girls in America, taking in content that seems intended to make you hate your body is an adolescent rite of passage. The medium changes but the ritual stays the same. Before American girls' confidence was commodified by Instagram, it was at the whim of magazines filled with impossibly slender, airbrushed models and ads from industries relying on girls and women for revenue. At the core of this marketing, the message endures: you are riddled with flaws and imperfections. We will tell you what to buy, and what to do, to fix yourself . . . To some extent, the way these dynamics play out on Instagram is just a natural extension of how girls are treated in our culture anyway. The body positivity movement may have helped, but girls still internalize the message that part of their success in life will rest upon their ability to be admired for their appearance. Instagram measures and gamifies that — creating a virtual high school cafeteria as global as the 'explore' button, one that's peopled by countless unreal bodies.[2]

Crouse's analysis rings true to my own experience navigating the world of Instagram. Throughout the bulk of teenagehood, Instagram was a crucial source of internal value and self-worth. The perfectly curated images that I posted on my feed were consumed, perceived, judged and rated by my peers. I would meet up with girlfriends and we would carefully choose our outfits, matching the colours and the jewellery and the make-up and hair. By way of ritual, we would take turns posing, adjusting the lighting and our bodies, whilst we took hundreds of pictures to capture that one immaculate shot where we became flawless portraits of perfect faces, legs and cleavage. We'd rack our brains for song lyrics or quotes and heart emojis to create captions that told the world that we were cool, carefree, effortlessly candid and beautiful. My insecurities were offset by the streams of likes, comments and shares by my peers. There was an overwhelming pressure and competition to pursue and perform 'hotness'; to show that you're attractive, desirable, popular and liked, to commodify your image for the attention of your peers. The fewer clothes we wore, the more likes we received, whilst external validation was gained. I began to directly correlate my value, my worth in this world as a multifaceted complex human, with the number of likes I would receive on an Instagram picture. Social media for me was a paralysing and psychologically crippling addiction. If a picture that I posted didn't achieve a certain number of likes it would directly affect my mood. The spiralling would commence, my anxiety would heighten and the internal critic would emerge, vicious, ruthless and unforgiving. In her book *Girls & Sex*, American journalist Peggy Orenstein wrote about how social media reinforces the relentless externalisation of girls' sense of self.

> There is evidence that the more concerned a girl is about her appearance, weight, and body image, the more likely she is to consult a magic mirror of her social media profile, and vice versa: the more she checks her profile, the more concerned she becomes about appearance, weight, and body image. Comments on girls' pages, too, tend to focus disproportionately on looks, and even more than in the real world, that becomes a measure of friendship, self-image, and self-worth.[3]

Instagram, TikTok and Facebook are platforms that facilitate and enable this exchange of currency, where likes and comments cultivate social hierarchies translating into real-life popularity or 'clout'. Adriana Manago, a researcher at the Children's Digital Media Center in Los Angeles whose work focuses on adolescents' and young adults' behaviour on social media, claims that young people are beginning to understand and talk about themselves as a 'brand'.[4] Many young people are constructing their identities entirely from an external image which has been carefully curated and packaged online to be judged, approved and validated by their peers instead of viewing themselves as autonomous individuals who can build their identities from within, based on their needs, desires, and preferences. It almost seems as if they have resigned themselves to becoming a product, a product that has been made possible at the expense of their own internal sense of self.[5] In a patriarchal culture, as the subordinate gender, women are socialised to constantly compete, compare and undermine one another. This interaction, the act of comparison, is accelerated on social media as we are constantly exposed to the images of other women and girls who are ceaselessly posing, pouting and one-upping one another. These images are not always real; increasingly, they are not an accurate reflection of the complexity, difficulty, hardship and struggle that people experience in real life. On social media, individuals advertise the best possible version of themselves. Unreal, glossy snap-shots of reality, images that are often edited, manipulated and Photoshopped. Impossible and unobtainable beauty standards of plumped lips, unblemished faces, snatched waists, perky boobs and cellulite-free bums are achieved through rounds of expensive and painful beauty treatments. Botox, fillers, injections, facelifts, nose jobs, liposuction, tummy tucks, breast enhancements, hip reductions and Brazilian butt lifts are cosmetic procedures and surgeries that many celebrities and influencers have but often choose not to disclose.

My generation is a slave to social media. Losing a phone is like losing an arm. There is no distinction or separation between the real world and the virtual. It is non-stop. In February 2021, a survey conducted by American think tank

Pew Research Center found that 96 per cent of American children who are high school age or younger own a cellphone.[6] A 2020 survey of 2,167 five- to sixteen-year-olds in the UK found that 53 per cent of youngsters owned mobile phones from around the age of seven. The same report showed that by secondary school phone ownership was 'almost universal' and that phones 'dominate children's lives'.[7] We are living in an image saturated culture that entices teenage girls and boys to spend hours and hours scrolling on their phones to browse the lives of their peers every waking day. We are now living much of our lives in a digital world that is not real, where we are constantly perceiving and being perceived, judging and being judged. Where there is an invisible but inescapable pressure to be constantly visible. 'Visibility these days seems to somehow equate to success,' declared Michaela Coel in her winning speech at the 2021 Emmys.

We scroll, we judge, we compare, we post, we scroll, we judge, we compare, we post. This is, for many young people, a never-ending spiral of addiction to a spinning carousel of comparison, judgement, jealousy and insecurity. Writing in the *Atlantic*, journalist Derek Thompson deemed it 'attention alcohol', explaining, 'Like booze, social media seems to offer an intoxicating cocktail of dopamine, disorientation, and, for some, dependency.'[8] Teenagers are constantly bombarded with online content of perfection, sending the implicit messages that translate in many young minds as a ceaseless reinforcement that they are not 'good enough', 'pretty enough', 'skinny enough', 'productive enough' or 'strong enough'.

Human beings were not designed to live in this way. We are navigating an ever-expanding tide of exposure to the judgement of others, a world where young people are sourcing their self-worth from Instagram likes and TikTok views. It's an exhausting life that we now lead; with immediate and unlimited access to one another, we develop unhealthy patterns of behaviour such as the stalking of exes, obsessions with models and influencers that live apparently idyllic, problem-free lives online. We know what everyone's doing, wearing and eating all the time. According to research published by the Royal Society for Public Health, Instagram has the most negative impact on young people's mental well-being of all social networks.[9] Leaked internal research conducted by staff at the Facebook company (now rebranded as Meta) who own Instagram has repeatedly found that it is harmful to young users, particularly teenage girls. One such presentation, from 2019, found that 'thirty two percent of teen girls said that when they felt bad about their bodies, Instagram made them feel worse'. Another internal report argued that 'aspects of Instagram exacerbate each other to create a perfect storm', claiming the pressures to look perfect and share only the best moments lead teenagers to depression, low self-esteem and eating disorders.[10] Yet despite the toxicity and the harmful impact on young people, the show goes on for big tech in the pursuit of profit with lots of cash at stake here. A spokesperson for the 5Rights Foundation called for a change in the way these companies conduct their businesses. 'In pursuit of profit these companies are stealing children's time, self-esteem and mental health, and some-times tragically their lives . . . This is an entirely human-made world, largely privately owned, designed to optimise for commercial purposes – it does not have to be like this. It is time to optimise for the safety, rights and wellbeing of kids first – and then, only then – profit.'[11] Shortly after these comments, Facebook's founder, Mark Zuckerberg, was accused by whistleblower Frances Haugen of 'putting astronomical profits before people'. In October 2021, Haugen told a US Senate hearing that Facebook's platforms 'harm children, stoke division and weaken our democracy'. Body image problems, eating disorders and body dysmor-phia are all by-products of a social media culture that equates external appearance with intrinsic value. Social media accelerates a pre-existing and age-old ideology of beauty as a woman's most defining feature, more important than what's inside, more important than our real-life achievements, intellectual capacity and personality traits, such as empathy, strength, courage, independence and kind-ness, which help us live meaningful and fulfilling lives.[12]

Taking time away from social media has been transforma-tive in my own life. I have found harmony with myself again, I feel engaged in the world around me, and my self-worth and confidence have improved significantly. I think there is so much to be gained in breaking these habits, in putting the screens away, in quieting the noise, in deleting those apps for a little while. At an event I attended in London, I heard writer Elif Shafak speak about how there is an important distinction to be made between 'information' and authentic 'knowledge' in this digital age. Tweets, Instagram infographics and Reddit threads are all sources of information, but books, journals, research papers and slow journalism are mediums that will empower you with real knowledge. By being away from a screen, your concentration levels could improve, you might become more disciplined, expand your interests, develop your intellectual curiosity or discover new hobbies. Most importantly, what you will gain is time. You will have more time to actually live in the real world. As a teenager, I think my average screen time was a disturbing seven to eight hours a day. Instead, go outside, meet up with your friends, get on a plane, dance at a concert, learn a new recipe, go for a run, meditate, read a book! You won't regret it.

The Best Men Can Be

In January 2019, Gillette, the men's razor company, released an advertisement entitled, 'We Believe: The Best Men Can Be', playing upon its previous slogan, 'The Best a Man Can Get'. The advertisement features news clips of the #MeToo movement, scenes of sexism and harassment in the workplace and in films, and videos of violence between young men and boys. 'We believe in the best in men,' intones the voiceover, 'to say the right thing, to act the right way. Some already are, in ways big and small. But "some" is not enough, because the boys watching today will be the men of tomorrow.' The latter half of the advert features videos of men holding each other accountable for predatory or aggressive behaviour as they intervene to stop friends from catcalling, bullying and fighting. The advert advocates for a positive form of masculinity, showcasing caring and empathetic men, who champion kindness and consideration whilst discouraging their peers from violence and harassment.

Immediately, the advert went viral, amassing more than four million views on YouTube in forty-eight hours. It was polarising. The response was initially lavish praise and furious complaint, which was then quickly replaced by an overwhelming negative backlash despite the messages of compassion and tolerance.[1] I remember watching the advert when it came out and reading the outraged comment section. I felt a deep sense of anxiety and sadness. I could not put two and two together: the messages of empathy and kindness with the eruption of hate and anger. I was speechless. How could this two-minute clip provoke such an extreme response in people? What was it about this advert that goaded such anger, such hatred and such defensiveness? Why was the response so polarised?

The comment section rapidly descended into a cultural battleground, with negative responses viewing the advert as an 'assault on masculinity' that blamed all men for 'the actions of a few'. Countless men and some women pledged on social media to boycott Gillette and dump their razors. Others blasted the company for 'gender shaming men' and for 'crapping all over the guys' who have supported their company for decades. Outspoken British journalist and presenter Piers Morgan tweeted, 'I've used @Gillette razors my entire adult life but this absurd virtue-signalling PC guff may drive me away to a company less eager to fuel the current pathetic global assault on masculinity. Let boys be damn boys. Let men be damn men.'[2] Australian journalist Andrew P. Street tweeted, 'The comments under the @Gillette toxic masculinity ad is a living document of how desperately society needs things like Gillette toxic masculinity ad. Seriously: if your masculinity is THAT threatened by an ad that says we should be nicer then you're doing masculinity wrong.'[3]

This idea that 'masculinity' can be defined and approached differently is echoed by the head of policy, research and innovation for the Family Initiative, Duncan Fisher. He wrote that the advert offered many men an alternative 'voice' from the widely accepted traditional framework of masculinity. 'There are a lot of men who want to stand up for a different type of masculinity, but for many there has not been a way for men to express that – we just need to give them a voice. Obviously this is an advert created by an agency to sell razors but it represents an attempt to change the dialogue'.[4] The *Oxford English Dictionary* defines masculinity as 'the fact of being a man; the qualities that are considered to be typical of men'. It is a set of attributes, behaviours and roles associated with men and boys that is viewed by sociologists as social construction, existing not in objective reality but as a consequence of human interaction. To be clear, masculinity is not, by itself, inherently toxic. Strength, courage, independence, leadership and assertiveness are examples of traits that are traditionally seen as masculine in Western society. These traits alone are commendable and striving towards them can help both men and women lead rewarding lives with meaning and fulfilment. Part of what pushes stereotypically male traits such as confidence, self-sufficiency, strength, and assertiveness to become toxic is when they are reinforced by unrealistic societal expectations and pressures. In his TED talk, American actor Justin Baldoni explores how these societal expectations of men can make them feel like they're 'not enough'.

> I've been pretending to be a man that I'm not my entire life. I've been pretending to be strong when I felt weak, confident when I felt insecure and tough when really I was hurting. I think for the most part I've just been kind of putting on a show, but I'm tired of performing. And I can tell you right now that it is exhausting, trying to be 'man enough' for everyone all the time . . . I don't have a desire to fit into the current broken definition of masculinity, because I don't just want to be a 'good man'. I want to be a good human.

Baldoni shows how boys and men are victims of the pressures of performance, constantly having to maintain an appearance of 'hardness'. In our society, there is so much emphasis on 'being a man' and 'manning up'. It is an unrealistic pressure to constantly appear strong, hard, powerful, confident and assertive all the time, in every aspect of life. Writing on the implications of patriarchy on men and boys, American author and social activist bell hooks stated that,

> The first act of violence that patriarchy demands of males is not violence toward women. Instead patriarchy demands of all males that they engage in acts of psychic self-mutilation, that they kill off the emotional parts of themselves. If an

individual is not successful in emotionally crippling himself, he can count on patriarchal men to enact rituals of power that will assault his self-esteem.[5]

This reality, to me, as a woman, is desperately sad. Throughout my life, whilst at school and university, I have had endless conversations with friends about our feelings, emotions and mental health. We've discussed the ins and outs of everything from relationships, boys, parents and families, to our insecurities around body image, eating disorders and the pressures of social media. My friends and I have shown each other every part of ourselves, we've been vulnerable, sad, depressed and anxious together. We've shared our hopes, dreams, fears, and supported one another through break-ups, funerals, university exams, jobs and new beginnings. As a woman, I have always found community, solace and strength through sharing my feelings and emotional struggles with others. Knowing that I can seek support and openly confide with the people in my life has allowed me to evolve and grow as a human. I am able to confront toxic patterns of behaviour and become aware and accountable for my mistakes. Emotional dialogue and vulnerability within these relationships have given me solid ground in my most challenging moments and helped me heal in times of difficulty. Sharing openly keeps me sane; sharing openly has time and time again saved lives.

Too much pressure to perform 'masculine' traits stops men and boys from experiencing the vulnerability we all need to be human. It stifles their emotional openness and willingness to discuss their problems or to seek help from others when in need. Keeping up with these impossible expectations is exhausting and can be detrimental to one's mental health, well-being, self-worth and body image. Men are far less likely to discuss mental health problems with a medical professional, and if sexually abused, it can take decades before they feel able to disclose details of their sexual assault. Men may not feel able to talk about such abuse due to the stigma and shame that surround these experiences. Male survivors experience the same effects as other survivors but often face more extreme barriers to coming forward or reporting their experiences. We have received testimonies from men and boys on Everyone's Invited who detail both historic and recent abuse. They reveal how these incidents leave profound emotional and psychological scars as they struggle with anxiety, depression, post-traumatic stress disorder, flashbacks and eating disorders. Just like female survivors, male survivors also experience feelings of blame and shame in the aftermath of their trauma. Patriarchal pressures and an overemphasis on stereotypically masculine traits, such as strength and physical dominance in society, mean that many male survivors battle with the feeling that they are 'less of a man' as they were unable to fight back or stop the assault. Moreover, many victims experience confusion over their sexual orientation in the aftermath of sexual violence perpetrated by another man or boy and homophobia in society at large has prevented male victims from speaking out. Male sexual abuse is severely under-reported due to the enormous stigma that surrounds these experiences as well as harmful rape myths that exist in society, such as the idea that men can't be sexually abused. Another myth that prevents victims from acknowledging or reporting their experience is that men who become sexually aroused or have an erection must have wanted it or enjoyed it. When, in truth, both erection and ejaculation are physiological responses that can occur from unwanted physical contact or in moments of extreme stress.[6]

Any boy or man can be a victim of sexual assault regardless of their size, appearance, strength or sexual orientation. The Crime Survey for England and Wales (CSEW) estimated that 155,000 men aged sixteen to seventy-four had experienced a sexual assault or attempted sexual assault in the year ending March 2020.[7] According to research carried out in February 2021 for the charity Mankind UK, 14 per cent of people identifying as men had been coerced or pressured into sexual activity and 9 per cent said they had been raped or assaulted by penetration. The research suggests that about half of men have experienced a non-consensual or unwanted sexual experience.[8] Mankind demanded that the government develop a national sexual crimes strategy that takes a more inclusive approach in order to meet 'the needs of all victims of unwanted sexual experiences'. In 2020, the Office for National Statistics reported that males accounted for three-quarters of suicide deaths registered (3,925 registered male deaths compared with 1,299 female deaths).[9] Negative body image, depression, anxiety and the stifling of emotional openness are the result of the pressures men face in living up to these patriarchal, masculine ideals.

As they get older, men may experience debilitating feelings of isolation and loneliness in their day-to-day lives as they are unable to speak openly about their problems. These insecurities may manifest in a need to oppress others in order to feel the dominance and security that is their 'birthright' according to a patriarchal form of masculinity. This overcompensation can lead to misogyny, hate and abusive behaviour, namely, 'toxic masculinity'. The sexualisation and dehumanisation of women can be seen as a way to preserve 'masculinity'. This is the form of masculinity that does not allow boys to cry or speak openly about their mental health and it is the same form of masculinity that dehumanises and objectifies women.[10] Writing for the *Independent* in the wake of Wayne Couzens's conviction (the police officer who raped and murdered Sarah Everard), journalist Dearbhla Crosse highlights how sexist humour normalises and enables predatory behaviour and violence.

> 'Locker room banter' is the linguistic underbelly where chauvinism is cultivated and normalised. It's a privileged inner sanctum within which some men get to mask their thinly-veiled misogyny behind 'jokes' . . . Belittling women through humour makes male violence socially acceptable. Sexist jokes deflect from misogynistic intent, often providing a carte blanche to share prejudicial ideas. This feeds into a culture where predatory behaviour is overlooked.[11]

Sexism and outright misogyny in the form of sexist jokes and derogatory comments are by-products of toxic masculinity. Power is re-established in these smaller forms of oppression, or microaggressions, wearing down recipients by a thousand cuts. Growing up, this kind of behaviour was the norm amongst the groups I socialised with. Rape jokes and dehumanising comments were thrown around like party confetti. Predatory behaviour was normalised, boys and girls excused this behaviour with comments such as, 'He's a nice guy but just a bit weird with girls' and, 'He's just a bit rapey when he's drunk.' When we laugh at threatening behaviour or trivialise rape, we risk compounding narratives that 'devalue women and normalise male-on-female violence.'[12] When we fail to challenge this behaviour, not only are we enabling abuse, we are also letting men and boys down. How will they ever know that what they are doing is harmful if no one tells them that it is? When I spoke to a senior staff member at a school in London, she told me that her female pupils strongly believed that if the boys who were sexually harassing and bullying them were genuinely aware of the impact of their behaviour, they were sure that they would no longer keep doing it. Boys and men need opportunities to recognise where they've gone wrong, to face up to bad behaviour, and have the chance to change their ways and become accountable for their mistakes. If we want men and boys to be better and feel better we can't excuse 'locker room banter' or brush off sexual harassment anymore. We need to encourage men and boys to value empathy, to become in touch with their own vulnerability, to look out for others and hold their own friends accountable.

In October 2021, David Batty reported in the *Guardian* on a study conducted by the University of Kent that examined the psychological profiles of sexually violent male students. The study, 'Understanding Sexual Aggression in UK Male University Students', found that 'of the 554 male students surveyed, 63 reported that they had committed 251 sexual assaults, rapes and other coercive and unwanted incidents in the past two years'.[13] The article goes on to say that there is

> a strong association between toxic masculinity and sexual violence, with those who reported committing offences also admitting to misogynistic views, such as believing that women who get drunk are to blame if they get raped, and having sadistic sexual fantasies about raping and torturing women. Such views and fantasising were not held by participants who did not report sexual misconduct and violence, the study noted.[14]

Responding to the study, Professor Nicole Westmarland, director of the Durham Centre for Research into Violence and Abuse, asserted that,

> The association between rape supportive beliefs, negative attitudes towards women and actually committing acts of violence and abuse is one that has been demonstrated before

in research in US universities. This study shows the same to be the case in the UK and points to the need for universities to step up their focus on perpetrators while providing victims with the support and action they need following sexual assault.[15]

Batty also contacted Everyone's Invited for comment, to which we responded with the following:

We have always believed that sexist beliefs, misogyny and toxic masculinity lead to predatory behaviour. The importance of exposing rape culture across society should not be underestimated. Sexism is part of a continuum of violence and when any individual is dehumanised they become vulnerable to violence. Let's help men and boys to become well-informed role models who have the courage to be proactive, to call out behaviour and hold their friends accountable.

In this environment, these behaviours exist on a spectrum; 'sexism is part of a continuum of violence.'[16] It begins with degrading misogynistic language, rape jokes and 'get back in the kitchen' banter. It manifests online as teenage boys AirDrop each other 'nudes' during maths lessons and young girls receive unsolicited 'dick pics' from their peers. It escalates as beliefs and attitudes feed into action; stalking, voyeurism, groping, flashing and overt sexualisation. The endpoint of such misogyny is rape and murder, as seen in the case of Sarah Everard and countless other women who are murdered at the hands of men. According to Femicide Census, on average, in the UK alone, a man kills a woman every three days.[17] Dehumanising, predatory behaviour is about establishing power and dominance, it's about living up to the expectations of a patriarchal form of masculinity. A form of masculinity that the Gillette advert challenges, offering an alternative, a chance for men and boys to redefine what it means to be a man. To be 'the best men can be', to look out for others, to help those in need and to value empathy and respect. As Gary Coombe, then president of Global Grooming at Procter & Gamble, which owns Gillette, said, 'By holding each other accountable, eliminating excuses for bad behaviour and supporting a new generation working toward their personal best, we can help create positive change that will matter for years to come.' Reframing what it is to be a man isn't an attack on men. It's about helping them to reach their full potential as human beings, embracing all the parts of themselves and freeing them from the oppressive constraints of our society's narrow definition of masculinity. Boys and men need opportunities and safe places to share their humanity. Let's encourage them to talk openly about their feelings, have genuine, vulnerable conversations about their relationships, struggles, hopes and dreams.[18] Bernice King, youngest child of late civil rights activist Martin Luther King Jr, put it aptly when she said, 'This commercial isn't anti-male. It's pro-humanity.'

I Feel You Watching

I used to suffer anxiety attacks from worrying that sexy pictures I posted on Instagram as a teenager will at some point be 'exposed'. And that this somehow makes me unqualified, undeserving and unable to do the work that I do. In my nightmare, I am labelled as nothing but a 'bad role model' or 'slut', publicly ripped to shreds by the tabloids who relentlessly engage in the objectifying and brutalising act of shaming women in the public eye. A process that has, in the past, been lethal, an act of invasive scrutiny, an objectification and commodification. The relentless onslaught of women bashing in the UK tabloid culture eroticises female dehumanisation and degradation for profit. There is an overwhelming fear of exposure in the darkest depths of my being; a deep-seated, psychological state of paranoia. It is a feeling so strong, so powerful that, at times, I find myself unable to speak, unable to move. There is an invisible sense of compression; the feeling of air pressing me down from every direction, where my voice and my world and my life feel so small, so still.

I cringe at the thought of body shaming other women, or judging others for the choices they make about the way they decide to present their bodies both online and in the real world. As women, our faces, clothes and bodies are and have always been scrutinised, judged, dissected, objectified, exploited, commodified, sold and controlled. Who am I to add to this tired chorus of judgement? As singer Billie Eilish, who is known to speak out about body shaming and the relentless scrutiny of female bodies, intones in her spoken word piece 'Not My Responsibility'. The lyrics are preoccupied with the experience of being scrutinised by the world. The piece is a critique on the overbearing and suffocating microscopic scrutiny that modern women in the public eye are forced to endure. For Eilish, it is that the very act of existing, the fact of being, living beneath her skin, as a woman, is enough cause for public outrage and praise. The entire piece is preoccupied with the experience of being perceived, an external force pushing in on her from the outside. Her awareness of the scrutiny of others is acute as much of the piece revolves around direct questions posed to her audience; the watchers, the judgers, the ones with the opinions, an audience that holds her hostage, with the threat of cancellation imminent, keeping her in check, restricted with no leeway for the mistakes needed for growth, to develop, to be human. In all her liberation and wealth and success, it is this audience, this following, this fan base, that enforces a powerful oppression of self. A life lived in the confines of a panopticon prison, marooned on an unnatural island of screens, cameras, videos, images, paparazzi, a *Nineteen Eighty-Four*-esque state of immobility and inescapable surveillance. It is depressing to see how someone so huge is living a life so small. As is echoed in the words of another world-famous female musician, Adele, 'The bigger that your career gets, the smaller your life gets.'[1] Adele has also been subjected to relentless public discussion and dissection of her body image throughout the course of her career. Recently, her lockdown weight loss dramatically dominated media headlines. You only have to google 'Adele weight loss' to arrive at an abyss of headlines engaged in an endless discussion about her body. 'Adele looks slimmer than ever after weight loss in fresh update',[2] '5 tips we can learn from Adele's amazing weight loss',[3] 'Adele's holiday photos spark debate on weight loss',[4] 'I'm a little bummed that Adele lost weight',[5] 'Adele weight loss: Singer shows off staggering transformation in new snap'.[6]

Adele and Eilish are just two examples of an archaic plight taken to an alarming extreme in the modern digital age. The body of a woman, discussed, dissected and judged, in a manner so invasive, reduces the physical form to a mere object. This has been the burden of womanhood throughout time, as women are perpetually regulated, controlled and consumed by men. Their movements restricted, their bodies belonging not to themselves but to private or public ownership. As Rebecca Solnit writes in her book *Wanderlust*, 'In Middle Assyria (circa the seventeenth to eleventh centuries BC), women were divided into two categories. Wives and widows "who go out unto the street" may not have their heads uncovered, said the law; prostitutes and slave girls, contrarily, must not have their heads covered.'[7] Visible discrimination in the enforcement of prescribed ways of dressing can be seen in the scrutiny placed on however much or little of women's bodies and faces are covered or uncovered, something modern society engages with on a daily basis. In 'Not My Responsibility', Eilish claims that when she wears 'what is comfortable' then she is 'not a woman' but if she sheds the layers she is deemed 'a slut'. Her bold choices of dress reflect these comments in her signature baggy, oversized looks, which conceal every inch of her body, and the contrasting Marilyn Monroe old-Hollywood-inspired corset look that she wore on the cover of British *Vogue*, which accentuated her cleavage and curves. Both looks, despite representing the two extremes, have elicited contradicting public outrage and praise. In a world where women have been socialised to please and seek approval, a paradoxical state of affairs emerges where winning is impossible. Visible discrimination is also explored in Margaret Atwood's feminist dystopian novel *The Handmaid's Tale*, where women are regulated, controlled and oppressed in a totalitarian theocracy called Gilead. They are sorted into categories by the patriarchal elite – including Wives, Handmaids, Marthas, and Econowives – shown through the modest colour-coded uniforms. Atwood calls her novel a work of 'speculative fiction', meaning that everything described in it is grounded in historical precedence. She drew inspiration from the Islamic revolution in Iran in 1978-9 that saw a theocracy established where the rights of women were dramatically curtailed, and women were strictly controlled and endured an enforced visible discrimination as the new Islamic authorities imposed a mandatory dress code that required the wearing of the hijab.

Though these examples seem extreme, the threads and themes remain pertinent to this day. In *Wanderlust*, Solnit highlights that society, with its prevalence of routine sexual harassment, implicitly suggests that women who walk, 'walk not to see but to be seen,'[8] that they exist not for themselves but for others, and that their bodies are not their own but considered objects in both the public and private spheres. No matter what we wear or how we act, there will always be judgement, criticism and shame. Growing up, the threat and possibility of violence was implicit in the aggressive propositions, catcalls, whistles, leers, comments, crude gestures, groping, grabbing and following in public spaces. In all forms of attire, be it jeans, shorts, tracksuits, miniskirts or school uniform, women, especially young women, cannot escape sexual harassment. On the implications of public sexual harassment, Solnit quotes an unnamed scholar who observed,

that women will not feel at ease, that we will remember our role as sexual beings, available to, accessible to men. It is a reminder that we are not to consider ourselves as equals, participating in the public life with our own right to go where we like when we like, to pursue our own projects with a sense of security.[9]

These discriminatory assertions of power, designed to minimise and objectify, imbued in me, as they have in most women, a lingering sense of paranoia that felt like the soundtrack to my existence. The fear of violence, and rape, and murder, especially in the wake of the deaths of Sarah Everard, Bibaa Henry, Nicole Smallman, Sabina Nessa and the countless other women who men have murdered in public spaces, forces women off the streets and into their homes. Dependence replaces independence as male protectors and material barriers are relied upon to safeguard women from sexual threat.[10] As a twenty-three-year-old woman, I experience significantly less sexual harassment in my day-to-day life than I did throughout my teenage years. Young women and girls bear the brunt of these experiences, which is disturbing to consider. Teenagers are less sure of themselves, less experienced, less aware of boundaries and their rights and freedoms; they are easy targets.[11] Looking back, there are too many experiences to count. I blocked out these interactions as they happened, cultivating a mindset where I would focus my vision straight ahead, refusing to engage in or acknowledge what was happening in order to keep moving forward. I now understand this response to be a survival technique, a way of getting on without actually having to 'sit with' the feelings of shame, humiliation and self-awareness wrought by these everyday violations. Other survival techniques include: holding your keys so that they stick out from in between your fingers; opening the front door as quickly as possible when returning home late at night; pretending to be on the phone when walking in the dark; wearing or not wearing headphones; sharing your location with family and friends so they know where you are at all times; walking quickly or literally running down the street in fear of being followed; travelling in groups or pairs; avoiding public transport at night; crossing the street when you don't actually need to; running into a shop; wearing a fake engagement or wedding ring; saying you have a boyfriend in the hope you're left alone; cutting your hair very short or shaving your head (friends who have done this report that all forms of sexual harassment ceased immediately). The threat of imminent violence is so entrenched within girls and women that it's second nature to tell our friends to 'Text me when you get home' after leaving a venue on a night out.

How are young women expected to navigate the many confusing and contradictory messages they receive from birth? Appearing desirable and beautiful is a good thing, a source of power and validation we are told. But equally there are the messages of shame and victim-blaming around the body; imploring us to cover up, change our clothes, to compress, restrict, and suppress ourselves, become invisible. To be both Madonna and whore all at once. To be chaste, innocent, pure, but also sexy, wild, desirable. This is the bane of our existence. Women, no matter who we are, what we do, what we wear, or how we act, are burdened with a perpetual tide of scrutiny and judgement – a powerful enforcement of oppression, as women throughout history were and in the present day are forced to submit to both extremes – to completely cover up or to strip down to the bone.

When I posted pictures as a teenager, I wanted to be seen by my peers. I wanted to be accepted, validated, loved. I wanted the approval, the attention from boys my age, and I wanted to feel beautiful. The likes and the views and the comments gave me that – they gave me a kind of power in a world where I felt powerless. I think there is a gulf between the way we perceive ourselves and how we are perceived by others, especially as young people. At the time, I didn't really think about who was looking at these pictures. Yes, there is great strength in feeling positive about your body but it's more complicated than that, isn't it? When the predatory men, the creepy older men, the men who abuse their power are viewing these pictures and choose to believe that I desire their attention when I don't, what, then, is the way forward?

Objects

Why can't we do what we want? Wear what we want? And be who we want? Why can't I be 'sexy'? And isn't being 'sexy' a liberation? Isn't 'sexy' *empowerment*? In a world where the female body is subjected to constant judgement, relentless restriction, could the act of choosing to objectify one's body be a way of carving out power? An act of rebellion, a reclamation of control when you are made to feel so damn powerless? Or is the discourse of sexual empowerment obscuring a deeper sense of sexual disappointment or insecurity, a yearning for attention, validation, something as simple as the desire to be seen?[1]

My own experiences and those of my peers match up to what Peggy Orenstein uncovered in her interviews with young women. That wearing revealing clothing is simultaneously both a liberating and dehumanising experience. At home, getting ready with our girlfriends, we feel the power of 'hotness', amped up by the boss bitch mantra and the discourse of sexual liberation. But, as soon as we step outside, out into the real world, we are made to feel awkward, uncomfortable, we're stared at, objectified, catcalled, touched, groped, followed home and, most of all, shamed. Surely, in a world of patriarchal oppression there's genuine liberation in a woman's right to choose to look, to act and to dress however she desires? In *Girls & Sex*, Peggy Orenstein asks her readers if there is really such a thing as 'choice' in a hypersexualised, porn-saturated, objectifying, image-centred culture where it is not a choice but an imperative for women and girls to engage in a proliferative performance of 'sexiness'? Could it be that the imperative to self-objectify, to wear nothing more than a skimpy thong or bikini in order to be seen, valued and achieve success in a male-dominated, patriarchal society, is as oppressive as the enforcement of the veil; the act of covering up from head to toe? What is it to be empowered? When are we complicit and when are we defiant?[2] Who is the subject and who is the object? Am I exploiting a system of patriarchal oppression or is this system exploiting me? Diane Nguyen, a fictional character from the Netflix series *BoJack Horseman* (a wacky animated comedy populated by talking animals and a profound exploration of mental health, trauma and addiction), considers the life of another character, Sarah Lynn, who is a Miley Cyrus-type parody figure: child actress turned hypersexualised teen pop star who tragically dies young from a drug overdose. 'I do wonder as a third-wave feminist if it's even possible for women to "reclaim" their sexuality in this deeply entrenched patriarchal society. Or if claiming to do so is just a lie we tell ourselves so we can more comfortably cater to the male gaze?' she says.

The term 'male gaze' was first used by the novelist and art critic John Berger in his 1972 series of short films and subsequent book of the same name, *Ways of Seeing*. The 'male gaze' refers to the masculine heterosexual gaze through which women are displayed in the media, presenting them as sexual objects for the pleasure of the heterosexual male viewer. Berger distinguished between the 'surveyor' and the 'surveyed', 'as men look at women' and 'women watch themselves being looked at', arguing that both exist within women, a woman must 'continually watch herself' because 'how she appears to men is of crucial importance'. This is, according to his argument, because 'men survey women before treating them' thus 'how a woman appears to a man can determine how she will be treated'.[3] Berger envisions an inexorable surveillance of women, one which is both externally enforced and internally reinforced by the women themselves. Berger concludes that because 'the surveyor of woman in herself is a male' she therefore 'turns herself into an object – and most particularly an object of vision: a sight'.[4] While writers like Orenstein envision self-objectification as a conscious choice, Berger argues that the act of self-objectification is intrinsic to what it means to be a woman in this world. Berger's ideas were developed further by the film critic Laura Mulvey in her 1975 essay 'Visual Pleasure and Narrative Cinema'.[5] According to Mulvey, those who are looked at (women) are 'the bearer of meaning not the maker of meaning'. As men determine, control and interpret the actions of women in film, these women lack control over their own narrative and how they are seen and perceived by others (the other characters and the audience). The male gaze is then arguably inescapable. It's all around us, saturated in the media, in art, music and film, and deeply entrenched within women themselves; women know that they derive power and ascend faster in a male-dominated patriarchal society if they can successfully cater to it.

On the other hand, there is a form of distinctive power to be found in the distancing effect that renders a woman alien or other.[6] Women are idolised by men yet idols are nevertheless still objects to be looked at. Women in film, and in real life, exploit the power of sexuality to achieve what they desire. But at what point does this move beyond our control? At what point is this power no longer ours? And was it ever really ours to begin with? At what point are we serving a system that seeks to objectify us, to subordinate us, to turn us into lifeless objects of male desire? As a woman, at what point are you complicit in your own oppression?

• • •

For the bulk of my teenage years I was a staunch believer and proponent of the idea that performing 'hotness' or 'sexiness' equated to 'female empowerment'; a mainstream idea marketed, packaged and sold by countless female artists in a hypersexualised and exploitative entertainment industry.[7] Back then I would argue that women are exploiting the system to their gain. They are making millions, billions; they are economically empowered. They are 'choosing' to take part of their own free will; they are making the decisions and calling the shots, whether they're twerking in a thong on stage, performing a striptease around a pole in a music video or posing seductively, doe-eyed, shiny, oiled and slick on the cover of a magazine. I would say, again and again, they are reclaiming their sexuality in an industry and in a world that endlessly oppresses them, exploits them, takes advantage of them, profits from them – what could be more empowering than 'choosing' to sexualise and objectify themselves and then enjoying the profits of the commodification of their own sexuality? Cardi B has repeatedly cited her time as a stripper as a liberating source of economic empowerment that allowed her to escape poverty and domestic abuse. Similarly, model and entrepreneur Emily Ratajkowski, who appeared in the infamous 'Blurred Lines' video, in her debut collection of essays *My Body* views modelling as resigning to the object of 'mannequin', a strategic means to an end, a form of freedom in its ability to empower her economically, giving her the ability to travel, work and attain wealth.[8] She's 'playing the system', the patriarchal image-centred capitalist system of exploitation that we all exist in and have to make our way through. In *Girls & Sex*, Orenstein argues that despite the rise to fame, success, wealth and power, musicians, influencers and models who choose to objectify their bodies for profit are still operating in and upholding the same oppressive and exploitative system that forces women to look, behave and act in a very particular and restricted way in order to be heard, seen and successful in their work. Writing on self-objectification Orenstein, in consideration of the music industry, underscores the importance of not conflating this individual form of self-objectifying economic empowerment with meaningful, widespread and collective change for women.

> Artists such as Gaga or Rihanna or Beyoncé or Miley or Nicki or Kesha or Katy or Selena may not be puppets, but they aren't necessarily heroes either. They're shrewd strategists, spinning commodified sexuality as a choice, one that may be profitable but is no less constraining, ultimately either to female artists or to regular girls. So the question is not whether pop divas are expressing or exploiting their sexuality so much as why the choices for women remain so narrow, why the fastest route to the top as a woman in a sexist entertainment world (just as for ordinary girls on social media) is to package your sexuality, preferably in the most extreme, attention-getting way possible.[9]

There is an illusion to be had, an illusion that we so easily and literally buy into. An unobtainable standard, a non-inclusionary, attention-grabbing performance of 'hotness' to maintain, which, in the end, benefits these female celebrities – but only them – in a huge way. The individuals are catapulted to extreme wealth, power, status and career success. But this kind of power is reserved for the privileged, surgically enhanced, Beverly Hills-reigning, Lamborghini-driving few; women, as a group, do not collectively benefit from their individualised successes.[10] Emily Ratajkowski also explores this illusion in *My Body*. Although the subject of heavy criticism by many who point to her hypocrisy in her continual perpetuation of this unobtainable, objectifying standard of beauty displayed on her Instagram feed, I don't believe we should dismiss women who live in contradiction when so many of us do. Her essays, taken together, are ultimately not a justification or celebration of self-objectification and the exploitation of one's own sexuality for profit; but, in the end, something more painful, sad and difficult to stomach. It is an understanding and an acknowledgement of systemic abusive practices in the fashion and entertainment industries, the oppressive systems and the predatory men who have exploited, taken advantage of, and, in harrowing moments, abused her. She scrutinises the idea that self-objectifying empowerment has, in a sense, eased these systems of abuse in its implementation of a false consciousness, a misguided belief in agency and control, in the riskiest and most precarious spaces, in an industry defined by inequality. In the end, despite Ratajkowski's claim that the purpose of her book is to 'not arrive at answers but to explore ideas', she seems to be saying that in the many moments where she believed she held power, especially as a young impressionable model, she didn't, in fact, have any power, agency or control at all. Her essays struck a chord with my own experience as a teenager growing up in London and navigating the sexual landscape of my generation. Looking back, there were so many moments during my first sexual encounters where I believed that I was the one in control, that because I was 'empowered' I knew what I was doing. In the deeply sexist and misogynistic environment I grew up in, I felt powerful when I received immediate validation and attention from my peers for performing 'sexy' and 'hotness'. But, in practice, in the real world, this discourse of self-objectifying empowerment seems to have masked for me, and for many of my female peers, a deeper sense of at best sexual disappointment, and at worst pain and abuse, with a chaser of silence solidified by layers of shame. *Washington Post* journalist and writer Christine Emba wrote in her essay 'Consent Is Not Enough, We Need a New Sexual Ethic' (an excerpt from her book *Rethinking Sex: A Provocation*) that the modern sexual climate where 'there seems to be wide agreement among young adults that sex is good and the more of it we have, the better' has inadvertently led us to the point where 'consent' has become the disappointing baseline in our sexual culture. She argues that, when choosing to have sex with someone, consent is not enough and that kindness is important too. In response to Emba's essay, *New York Times* journalist Michelle Goldberg wrote that sex positive feminism has now, in recent years, become 'a cause of some suffering it was meant to remedy' and that, 'what passes for sex positivity is a culture of masochism disguised as hedonism. It's what you get when you liberate sex without liberating women.'[11] Growing up, I remember the overwhelming pressure on girls to be sexually open, to have lots of casual sex, and to try more extreme sex acts that they weren't necessarily comfortable with or ready to try. This was reinforced in the testimonies submitted to Everyone's Invited that recount moments where, imbued in them by the discourse of sexual empowerment, a false sense of sexual confidence pushed them into precarious scenarios where they no longer felt in control. Where boundaries were crossed and power was stolen. Leaving them, in the end, not with a feeling of power or freedom or intimacy or love but with a gaping emptiness that comes with the experience of being used.

Orenstein's work reminds us that there is an important distinction to be made between performing 'sexy' (online and in sexual relationships) and the actual experience and pursuit of sensuality, sexual pleasure and sexual exploration. She suggests that in these crucial early years, at this key juncture in their development, teenagers should have both the freedom and confidence to learn the foundational lessons of desire, consent, attraction, equal pleasure, arousal and intimacy in safe and non-judgemental settings. Yet, there seems to be a disconnect between how women and girls feel compelled to present themselves externally and genuine sexual expression, exploration and agency in their intimate experiences. To convey her point, she cites *Female Chauvinist Pigs*,[12] in which writer Ariel Levy offers a scathing critique of highly sexualised American culture where women are objectified, objectify one another and are ultimately encouraged to objectify themselves. This she calls 'raunch culture', which she deems as not 'progressive' or 'liberating' and 'not about opening our minds to the possibilities and mysteries of sexuality'. She notes the 'disconnect' between 'hotness' and the sex itself. Levy takes the example of famed socialite and businesswoman Paris Hilton, viewing her as the ideal celebrity in a culture that values the appearance of sexiness over sex itself. She points out that during her leaked sex tape, Paris seems bored, uninterested and unaroused, to the extent that she takes a phone call in the middle of intercourse. The only moment where she appears engaged or excited is when she is posing for a picture. Hilton, in the past, has even said herself that, 'My boyfriends always tell me I'm not sensual. Sexy but not sexual.'[13] The disconnect is so strong that she herself isn't the one opening up about her sexuality: instead, she delivers second-hand comments from her boyfriends.

As a teenager, I remember having many conversations with my female peers who told me that sex felt like a chore, an act they felt ambivalent towards rather than an experience of genuine arousal, enjoyment or excitement. Some told me that they had never experienced an orgasm during intercourse with a sexual partner, whilst the boy, in almost every encounter, orgasmed without fail. Sex would always end when the boy came. The girls reported a sense of detachment, resembling an out-of-body experience, and, at times, a propensity to become inert during sex, just to see if he'd notice, to see if he was the slightest bit conscious of her presence as a sexual being with her own desires.

In the wake of the *Sex and the City* series revival *And Just Like That. . .*, the absence of Kim Cattrall's iconic character Samantha is painfully felt by both critics and fans. Having been a little too young during the series's heyday, I hadn't watched any of the original episodes, just the subsequent films, which came out years after the show ended. Since the premiere of the revival, I decided to give the original a chance and I have found myself drawn to Samantha's character. Samantha Jones, in the context of the nineties, is a representation of a modern, independent, sexually active woman. She exudes sensuality and embodies 'sexiness' not just in her external appearance and sexual confidence but also within her real sexual relationships where she takes unapologetic ownership of her desire and relentlessly engages in an exploration of her sexuality. She knows who she is, what she wants and what she likes. She embraces sex in a way that doesn't feel performative, but groundbreaking (for the time) and liberating. Although this show has many flaws – including scores of problematic moments that haven't aged well – back then there was something captivating in Samantha's character that looked and felt like an authentic representation of sexual empowerment, one where sexiness exists in parallel with the sex itself. It must be noted that this is, of course, at the end of the day, just a TV show, ultimately a performance delivered by an actress on the screen. And yet, it was a culturally influential representation of a confident woman with a liberating autonomous sexuality, setting a new standard and offering an alternative representation of female sexuality, a foil to her onscreen peer Charlotte's traditional and old-fashioned form of love and romance.

However, in recent years the idea that women must have lots of casual sex and many sex partners has entered the mainstream which has created, for some, a sense of pressure to meet sexual standards or expectations that might not be in tune with our own. Candace Bushnell, the real-life Carrie Bradshaw who wrote the column for the *New York Observer*, which was adapted into the *Sex and the City* anthology, said that, 'I think one of the worst things for women is that they've been divided into, "I'm wholly sex positive, and I'm up for anything" or "I'm a prude, and I'm saving it for my husband".' Now, 'there's so much pressure on women to have sex and enjoy it'. Agency is the key, she insists.[14] Not everyone is a Samantha; could this pressure be diminishing to our true desires and sexual needs?[15] Has this pressure, for some, become more restricting than liberating? I think everyone has different needs and has their own relationship with their body, the danger exists when we force ourselves to conform to culturally enforced sexual expectations that don't necessarily fit in with what we want or with what actually makes us feel good.

One big criticism of the original show is the gaping absence of inclusivity and diversity amongst the lead characters, in a TV show set in one of the most ethnically diverse cities in the world, New York. The show's representation of beauty is non-inclusionary as the four main characters are white, thin, privileged and mostly adhere to the Western beauty standard. It plays into all the typical problematic stereotypes by sidelining the LGBTQ+ community and people of colour characters as the gay best friends, othering prostituting drag queens and peddling racial stereotypes such as 'angry Black women', 'fiery/crazy Latinos', and hypersexualised Black men. The sexual scripts delivered by this show, whilst groundbreaking for their time, are limited, in their centring of whiteness onscreen. Yet, it seems that not much progress has been made since that time. Yes, there is the body positivity movement, pioneered by cultural figure-heads like singer and musician Lizzo, and actor and activist Jameela Jamil – whose Instagram community and podcast 'I Weigh' stands for radical inclusivity – which may well have made some meaningful strides in empowering individuals who don't fit the hypersexualised, 'slim thicc', blemish free, script of the day to feel confident in their bodies. It does ultimately seem, though, as driven forward by the perpetual onslaught of immaculate, toned and Botoxed bodies featured heavily throughout mainstream porn, social media, music videos, films and TV that these scripts are still relatively narrow and still overwhelmingly focused on image alone, on what we look like, on how we are appearing, on how we are presenting to the outside world, both in public and in intimate scenarios.

At the time of the song's release, I defended and loved Cardi B and Megan Thee Stallion's smash hit 'WAP', it felt as glorious as it was outrageous. I backed Kim Kardashian and I believed in Miley Cyrus. I loved Cyrus's journey, the transition from teen queen pop sensation chastity-ring-wearing era to her coming of age 'I am now a woman so allow me to be one' moment, right through to the stripping down gyrating on a foam finger at the VMAs, to the Malibu beach-hopping pixie-dancing time, to now, her cultural rebirth into the brilliance of the Bowie-inspired fully fledged, astonishingly talented, voice belting out 'Rock Star'. When I look at these women, I see complex, multifaceted beings who have existed in, and been forced to navigate and operate in, a highly sexualised, attention-grabbing and objectifying industry. How they present themselves does have an impact, they do have wide audiences and thus significant cultural influence but, ultimately, they are products of a culture we have all created, collectively, as a society. People criticise the Kardashians, dismissing them as nothing more than bad role models in promoting self-objectification online and in perpetuating unobtainable beauty standards, yet we can't stop watching them, consuming them, reading about them, scrutinising them and gossiping about their lives. This is a culture we all exist in, a culture we are all a part of and have a responsibility in upholding. They may present as the objects because we, the audience, are the voyeurs and the consumers who ceaselessly buy into their image. And so the system and the cycles and this culture continue to prevail and the ideology of 'image' endures.

Coming to terms with how the self-objectifying performance of 'hotness' may be very limited as a form of empowerment is difficult to stomach. Understanding that performing sexy might not actually match up to true sexual desire, sexual exploration, or the pursuit of genuine sexual pleasure may be a rude awakening for many young people.[16]

· · ·

As a young person, as someone who believes in sexual openness, freedom and the importance of agency and sexual pleasure in intimate relationships, these are uncomfortable ideas to consider. I have an impulse towards freedom, an impulse to defy any form of restriction. But is the new form of 'sexual liberation', the imperative to self-objectify and perform 'sexy' for your followers, a new order of restriction and oppression? In this day and age, posting a thirst trap[17] isn't groundbreaking or transgressive, especially when every other fifteen-year-old, TikTok star, influencer and celeb is doing the same thing. When image is everything, when likes on an Instagram bikini pic are the sole source of your self-worth, confidence and value as a human being, when looking sexy supersedes the pursuit of actual sexual pleasure in intimate relationships, there is a serious problem with the state of our culture.

When and where as women in a deeply patriarchal culture that is grounded in centuries of female subordination, oppression and control are we really free? How can we know what we really want? And what we truly desire? In the *Robber Bride*, writer Margaret Atwood argues that male fantasies are inescapable. Atwood questions whether male fantasies are ubiquitous, whether we can ever escape them: 'You are a woman with a man inside watching a woman. You are your own voyeur.'

Her observations are damning and difficult, underscoring the life of a woman as a life devoid of agency and autonomy. The male gaze, so deeply ingrained it lives inside, under the skin, a perpetual imposition, influencing every action and every move. Women prioritise their image because image is currency which affords them a kind of power, albeit limited, in a world where men rule. Catering to the male gaze is a means to an end for many women. A way in which we advance and ascend in a social order where men, overwhelmingly white men for that matter, continue to inhabit the vast majority of the most privileged positions in the economic, political and social spheres, both historically and in the present day. As Simone de Beauvoir once said, 'Representation of the world, like the world itself, is the work of men; they describe it from their own point of view, which they confuse with the absolute truth.'[18] And in 1948, she observed that 'humanity is male and man defines woman not in herself, but as relative to him; she is not regarded as an autonomous being . . . He is the subject, he is the absolute – she is the other.'[19] Whilst women are socialised to become objects for viewing pleasure they are simultaneously chastised and ridiculed for engaging in the act of self-objectification.

There are people I know who feel as much, if not more, shame for sexual inexperience than those who feel the shame of 'promiscuity'. So are we to engage in this eternal balancing act? Never too much, never too little, never crossing the line. Always bending and adjusting and injecting to obtain a standard that we know is impossible. Always hating our bodies no matter what they look like, the extraordinary bodies that move us, make us, that empower us every single day to breath and swim and read and stretch and sprint. Always performing, always acting, always assuming the roles we are prescribed to the extent where we lose who we are, where we never find out. In a sense, teenagers who objectify their bodies and selves online are only enacting something that feels like an inevitable burden of womanhood. They are accelerating a cultural socially inscribed lesson that we have been taught for centuries. To be self-conscious, to develop in oneself the inescapable awareness of being seen, perceived and crucially surveyed, and thus, as in Berger's view, enacting an eternal surveying of the self and resigning to the 'object'.

We all live in contradiction, where our values are in constant tension with our decisions, behaviour and actions. We are all bad feminists. It feels impossible not to be, given the way society is evolving. We blame and we shame those who we think are 'ruining it' for the rest, and when we do so we too often objectify, dehumanise and humiliate. We are all guilty of perpetuating norms and ideals that have impacted others harmfully because we live in a society that has, from birth, socialised us to do so. Imperfect and in flux. Young and old. It's so hard to be human. It's so hard to get it right.

So, the question remains. What is true empowerment? What does it look like and how do we find it? If I had truly understood the influence of the male gaze as a teenager, I don't think I would have cared so much about what I looked like and what other people thought of me. Maybe I would have liked my body just the way it was, maybe I would have spent less time worrying about my Instagram feed and more time discovering new things as well as finding out what I wanted and who I wanted to become. Finding my voice.

Just a Joke

The words we use to communicate with one another are powerful. Language, and the way we use it, directly affects our experiences and our behaviour. Calling your friend a 'slut' isn't necessarily 'just a joke'. Though it may have left your tongue with relative ease, the word, if delivered in a derogatory way, will have an impact on the recipient who might experience acute feelings of humiliation or shame. 'Slut' might trigger a loss of confidence or make her self-conscious about the way she is dressing or acting or speaking. 'Slut' might impact the way she is viewed and treated by others. Will she have no one to sit next to at lunchtime? Will she struggle to find a partner in drama class? Or be considered 'easy' by the boys in the year above? And if something happens, will it be her fault because everyone knows 'she gets around'?

In his theory of 'language games', Ludwig Wittgenstein explored how words acquire their meaning from their use. He argues that actions are woven into words and that 'words are deeds', meaning that there are real-life consequences for the words we use. For instance, if we consider the implications of the words 'help', 'fire' and 'no', we know that these words provoke a response. They are soliciting, warning and forbidding. When we use words, we affect our surroundings and the lives of those who share the world with us.[1]

For example, the term 'violence against women', widely used by feminists and activists worldwide, is a passive construction. The perpetrator is absent, leaving only the victim present; there is no one committing the act of violence. The result is a shifting of accountability from those perpetrating the vast majority of violence onto the group who are overwhelmingly the victims of violence. Here, victim-blaming is subtle yet profound. Victim-blaming is pervasive throughout society, in the structures, the systems, the minds, the courtrooms – even in the language used by campaigners for women's rights there is victim-blaming, albeit implicit. The media is also notorious for spinning language to shift the perceptions of the public. This can be seen in how rape cases are presented and how sexual predators are portrayed, with victim-blaming featuring heavily in media narratives and headlines. We see this frequently in the media as the perpetrator vanishes from view as acts are described with an absence of an agent: 'Woman raped whilst walking through the park' or 'Man in his 40s pushed to the ground and raped on footpath' or 'Woman drank six Jägerbombs in ten minutes on the night she was raped and murdered'. Researchers Linda Coates and Allan Wade wrote that doing this will 'reformulate the victims into perpetrators (responsible for acts committed against them) and the perpetrators into victims (not responsible for their own actions)'.[2]

Bias is often in the perpetrator's favour as the act of rape is replaced with terms such as 'forced sex', 'non-consensual sex', or 'sex with a minor'. Examples of this in practice can be found in the headlines: 'Major GOP donor calls for Missouri GOP governor to resign over allegations of forced sex' and 'Underage girl forced to have sex with Prince Andrew, US court document claims'. Headlines like these frame the victim as an active participant, alleviating the perpetrator from his role as actor. In doing so, they soften a hard reality: the reality of rape. An underage girl is a child. Minors and children cannot consent to sex. This is rape. We need to call it rape. When rape is framed as a 'type of sex' we rationalise it and normalise it.

One pervasive example of the way language influences us is in the way people talk about sex and, in particular, the inextricable presence of violence in slang around hook-up culture. 'Do you think you're gonna bang?'; 'When did you smash?'; 'Did you beat?'; 'Did you fuck?'; 'We destroyed each other'; 'Nailed her last night'; 'Yeah, we screwed'; 'Did you hit that?' Violence is overtly implicit in the way we talk about sex. If sex is framed by violence it will inevitably influence the way we have it. Phrases like 'hitting a home run' or 'going to second base' situate sex in the realm of games and competition, reducing individuals to trophies and playthings, to objects without agency. We can't even talk about female genitals without evoking connotations of violence or dehumanisation. Even the word 'vagina' originates from late seventeenth-century Latin meaning 'sheath' or 'scabbard' (the case for a sword). When violence and sex are used interchangeably to both describe and characterise each other, violence is absorbed into our understanding of sex and bleeds into reality, into real sexual experiences. When we use violent language to characterise the act of sex we normalise violence in sex.

American research professor and author Brené Brown wrote that dehumanisation begins with language and is then followed by images. She highlights examples throughout history where this has occurred, noting that during the Holocaust the Nazis described the Jews as *Untermenschen*, meaning subhuman; calling them rats, depicting them as disease-carrying rodents in everything from newspapers and pamphlets to children's books. Brown also noted that, 'Hutus involved in the Rwandan genocide called Tutsis cockroaches. Indigenous people are often referred to as savages. Serbs called Bosnians aliens. Slave owners throughout history considered slaves subhuman animals.'[3] Michelle Maiese, professor of philosophy at Emmanuel College in Boston, wrote about dehumanisation as a process. She defines it as 'the psychological process of demonizing the enemy, making them seem less than human and hence not worthy of humane treatment'. Caroline Hickson, director of the International

Planned Parenthood Federation Europe Network, said that, 'Sexist language that makes light of male violence normalises a coercive and threatening environment for women.' A study conducted in 2017 that examined the effect of sexist humour on men's self-reported rape proclivity ('a self-reported measurement that demonstrates a man's willingness to rape a woman under the circumstance that they would not be discovered') reinforces these ideas. The study found that in trivialising sex discrimination, 'sexist humour leads to a norm of tolerance of sex discrimination'.[4] 'Sexist men exposed to sexist humour have reported greater tolerance of sexist events',[5] greater willingness to discriminate against women[6] and a greater tolerance of societal sexism.[7] The 2017 study revealed that 'men exposed to sexist humour have reported a greater propensity to commit sexual violence against women, including rape'.[8]

In light of all this, it is alarming to consider the array of popular culture, the films and music I grew up watching and listening to, that popularised and normalised a culture of dehumanisation. The level of entrenched misogyny is eye-watering; sexism and sexual violence were normalised and accepted, to the extent that we would not raise an eyebrow or blink an eyelid at the content. Content that has not aged well at all. Films and TV shows such as *American Pie*, *Superbad*, *Family Guy* and *Gossip Girl* were some of the most popular shows and movies throughout my teenage years; a seminal rite of passage for most teenagers of my age group. When speaking to an American male friend about sexism in popular culture he brought up *Family Guy*'s Glenn Quagmire, who was 'everyone's favourite character'. A sex-obsessed fiend, he was essentially a caricature of a sexual predator whose defining feature was his objectification and abuse of women. In the show, he regularly sexually harasses female characters, keeps Asian sex slaves in the boot of his pick-up truck, inappropriately makes advances to all his friends' wives and daughters, pursues young girls, commits paedophilia, and non-consensually records, spies on and stalks women, watching them through windows, over fences, behind curtains and in bathroom cubicles. *Family Guy* creator, Seth MacFarlane, infamously complained about Fox's censorship over a cutaway gag which goes as follows: Quagmire rapes Marge Simpson before murdering the entire Simpson family.

Seth Rogen films like *Superbad* (2007) and *The 40-Year-Old Virgin* (2005) were hugely popular when released, and considered cult classics even now. Yet they are also saturated with degrading jokes and an incessant objectification of women. In *Superbad*, the character of Seth, played by Jonah Hill, compulsively objectifies girls. The camera is often positioned at the character's eye level, combining both Seth's and Evan's gaze and the audience's as it zooms in on Evan's mum's chest or Nicola's thong. At no point throughout this film does the camera present the point of view of any women.[9] The language used in the script's stage directions (penned by Rogen and Evan Goldberg) is profoundly marked by scopophilia (meaning 'the love of looking' and referring to the male gaze of Hollywood cinema) and explicitly captures and enacts the objectification of female bodies as the character of Fogell is viewing 'the ass of Nicola' who is described as an 'incredibly hot girl', a 'little skanky' and exuding 'sexual vibes' and wearing a 'black G-string', which can be seen through 'tight white pants'. Language rich in the discourse of objectification directs the action onscreen, the moving images, what we see when we watch the film in real time. But not just any film, a classic of the genre, a cult coming-of-age, iconic rite-of-passage of significant cultural influence, setting the norms, standards and social codes, encouraging, normalising and sanctioning it all. In *The 40-Year-Old Virgin*, dialogue includes jokes about hunting down 'drunk chicks. Don't confuse that with tipsy. We're talking about drunk. I want vomit in the hair. Bruised-up kneecaps. Broken heels is a plus.'

In May 2021, Rogen was interviewed by journalist Decca Aitkenhead in the *Sunday Times* and questioned about the voyeuristic and objectifying content in films like *The 40-Year-Old Virgin* and how they are now received in a post #MeToo era. His response went as follows: 'I would say that is something that is unfortunately representative of a very real mentality, but not something that we would be making comedy about, by any stretch of the imagination, any more. I look at that and think, yeah, that is not something we'd be doing today.' *Representative of a very real mentality* – perhaps Rogen has a point here. People who think like this, who behave like this, who hold views like this, do exist. They are real; it is a representation of culture that is still prevalent amongst some men and some boys. So, would it be right to silence or censor art or language that is representative of real life, real people, 'a very real mentality'? In the 2007 film *Knocked Up*, which Rogen also stars in, one character creates a database of the precise time stamps of where female nudity happens in the films he watches. Aitkenhead, in her write-up of the Rogen interview, concludes, 'If teenage boys were supposed to see that this made his character a jerk, I'm pretty sure the inference went over their heads. I think what they saw is that this is how their favourite movie star talks and thinks about women.'

This dilemma is by no means new. Should we censor art and language? Do we separate the art from the artist? To what extent does art have a stake in the real world? Does it impact real life? What about freedom of speech? These questions have been asked and re-asked and asked again and feel ever more pertinent in a digital age of polarisation, cancel culture and virtue-signalling.

• • •

Rap, hip-hop and drill music are some of the most contentious and hotly debated genres for their popularising and normalising of misogyny and sexism through problematic lyrics, objectifying music videos and the glamorisation of drugs and violence. Misogyny, both in its lesser and more extreme forms, emerges as ubiquitous and enduring in this genre, spanning though the '90s to the early 2000s, the 2010s and to the present day, originating in the US and expanding to global influence as the genre adapts and evolves in many countries across the world. Who could forget one of Kanye West's most famous lines referencing his high-profile feud with Taylor Swift where he raps about how he thinks he could have sex with her, calling her a 'bitch' who he made famous. And perhaps most notorious of all for the violence and aggression in his music and lyrics is Eminem, who is famous for rapping about choking, beating and murdering his wife, who he refers to as a slut and a whore.

Disturbing, yes. Frightening, yes. Violent, yes. The subject matter is dark but life was, for Eminem, turbulent. He had a disturbingly violent and deprived upbringing. His art is a reflection of his life, a life marked by poverty, suffering and abuse. Artists, those who came before him and those who have followed, make art about the worlds they navigate, their struggles and their pain. It has been, for many, a way out, an ascent to greatness or – purely out of necessity – a method of survival. In his podcast that grapples with this debate, award-winning spoken word artist, poet and rapper George Mpanga, also known as George the Poet, said that 'telling your own story is the secret to survival'.[10] Although we are better able to understand the origins behind such violence in a person through assessing their background and upbringing, the trauma and suffering are never a justification for violence.

In the UK, over the last five to eight years, drill music, a subgenre of rap originating from South Side, Chicago, has entered into the mainstream. The sound of drill is heavy and ominous, there is an urgency and an anger that breeds lyrics saturated with narratives of gang life; the selling of drugs, violence on the street and a culture of misogyny. Over the years, drill has become increasingly controversial, with police and politicians alike deeming the genre as a glamorisation of extreme criminal violence that both incites and provokes inner city gang warfare in real time. Jermaine Goupall, a fifteen-year-old student at St Joseph's College, was fatally stabbed seven times in south London on the evening of 8 August 2017 by twenty-one-year-old Adam Benzahi, eighteen-year-old Samuel Olivier-Rowland and seventeen-year-old Junior Simpson, who were all convicted of murder and given life sentences. The court heard that drill lyrics, penned and performed by Simpson, aka drill artist M-Trap, foreshadowed and predicted the fatal attack. This case was influential as one of the first murder cases to suggest a direct link between drill music and real-time violence.[11] Whilst the judge claimed that the lyrics were 'just for show', Goupall's father said that drill music possesses a 'demonic mindset'. Many, however, defend the genre, arguing that drill, emerging from the most disadvantaged and deprived communities, is unfairly demonised. Many have asked why Black musical forms are harassed by the authorities yet the violence and misogyny in rock music are given a free pass. Ciaran Thapar, a London-based youth worker and activist, wrote in the *Guardian* in 2019,

> Instead of muzzling what drill is trying to tell us, we need to see it as a rich, organic resource with which impactful conversations between educators and the most anxious, angry young people can be mined. In my youth work I have seen the sort of trust-building that can take place when drill is discussed under critical supervision. Only once a suitable dialogue has been established can the music's horrific content, and the warped morals of lyricists who fetishise knives, or are misogynistic, or brag about life in the trap house, be sustainably challenged. Demonising music in isolation of any other cushioning measures will push the darkest ideas explored in drill's unforgiving verses further out of reach of those of us who are trying to make real change on the frontline.[12]

Thapar is championing the importance of conversation, dialogue and empathy. Reaching out, working with young people, engaging them in the conversation, building in them an understanding, a deeper and wider perspective about the impact of their actions is fundamental if you want to change damaging behaviour and help young people lead more fulfilling and rewarding lives that are free from violence. Perhaps we should also be asking questions that scrutinise the wider social and political forces at play, the entrenched systems of structural racism and inequality that position young

Black and minority ethnic communities in an environment where such violence is a reality.

Misogyny in music has existed in all genres throughout history, as art is often a reflection of the norms and values of the time period. Mick Jagger and Keith Richards of the Rolling Stones have admitted that they are now no longer proud of the lyrics in their 1971 hit 'Brown Sugar', which includes lines that describe a slave master whipping Black women at midnight. 'Run For Your Life' by The Beatles, written in the '60s, is a threatening song to an ex-girlfriend of John Lennon's. He sings about how he would rather see her dead than with another man. 'More Than a Woman' by the Bee Gees (1977), from the iconic *Saturday Night Fever* soundtrack, is disturbing by today's standards because it feels paedophilic and predatory in tone. In recent years, Frank Loesser's Academy Award-winning holiday classic 'Baby, It's Cold Outside' (written in 1944) has fallen from favour with critics arguing that the lyrics edge closer to sexual harassment and date rape than innocent flirty fun. The song itself is a 'call and response' duet between a host or 'Wolf' performed by the male singer and a guest or 'Mouse' performed usually by a female singer. Yet, some historians have argued that the song is very much an authentic reflection of the rules and gendered roles of romantic pursuit of the time. Rachel Devlin, a professor of history at Rutgers University in New Jersey, wrote that it was a 'weird and contradictory time' where men were expected to push, and women were expected to make sure men didn't cross the line, which was entirely up to the women because if a line was crossed, and they did have sex, she was ruined. The song is an important historical document because it does represent these constant negotiations. It's describing an everyday encounter.[13]

Beth Bailey, author of *From Front Porch to Back Seat: Courtship in Twentieth-Century America* and a history professor at the University of Kansas, observed that the 'song comes from an era where women were just expected to say no, no matter what they wanted' and that, 'The culture refused to acknowledge women's right to say yes or no.' Looking back, it is fitting that the absence of consent in these lyrics falls in line with the cultural context from which the song emerges. If art reflects life, then it is without surprise that a song like Robin Thicke's 2013 'Blurred Lines' featuring T.I. and Pharrell Williams would become a smash hit, topping the charts of twenty-five countries, enjoying a twelve-consecutive-week streak at the top of the US Billboard Hot 100, and with its sales of 14.8 million cementing the track as one of the bestselling singles of all time.

Since its release, many music critics have deemed the phrase 'blurred lines' a glorification of rape culture. Ann Powers for NPR said that the lyrics objectify women and condone rape.[14] Annie Zaleski of *The A.V. Club* said that the song's 'old-man lecherousness and boys'-club friskiness comes off as uncomfortable and demeaning'.[15]

Spin magazine's Keith Harris believed the song to be 'a consensual two-way flirtation, a game both players get to win, with Thicke desperately launching goofball compliments at a woman who paws at him and prances away'.[16] The premiere of the song's infamous and highly controversial music video sent shock waves through the music industry, and skyrocketed lingerie-clad, animal prop-playing model Emily Ratajkowski to global fame. The video, directed by Diane Martel, features the near-naked models Ratajkowski, Elle Evans, and Jessi M'Bengue fawning over and dancing with clothed Thicke, T.I. and Williams. The topless models meow seductively at the camera, snuggling in bed with Thicke and riding stuffed animals whilst sticking their tongues out. The video also features a sign reading, 'Robin Thicke Has a Big Dick' spelt out in silver balloons. There was a significant backlash, a fierce reception dismissing it as misogynistic and offensive. Bertie Brandes of *Vice* called the video 'a masterpiece of idiocy and the level of stupidity and arrogance required in order for a video this banal, offensive and unimaginative is almost impressive. Except, it's not impressive at all, is it? It's ugly sexist uninspired bullshit dressed up as naughtiness, and it's creepy, creepy, creepy.' Initially, upon the video's release, an early twenties Ratajkowski defended the video saying that it wasn't sexist and it was made with a 'sarcastic attitude' and that she was secure in her body and nakedness on set. She, at the time, hailed it as a celebration of women and their bodies that promoted female confidence. Yet, in September 2015, in an interview with *InStyle*, Ratajkowski called the video 'the bane of my existence'. And in her 2021 collection of essays *My Body*, she reveals a darker side to the seemingly 'sarcastic' flirty fun, as she alleges that Thicke sexually assaulted her on set on the day of filming the video, suddenly groping her and cupping her bare breasts from behind. She writes that she tried to shake off the shock but that no one who witnessed it said anything. Despite being topless for most of the video, it was in that moment, she claimed, that she felt naked for the first time during the filming.

As Brené Brown and Ludwig Wittgenstein suggest, language has an impact in the real world – with real-world consequences arising from the words we use. The dehumanising lyrics followed by sexist imagery transform into Thicke's dehumanisation of Ratajkowski, his belief in his entitlement to her body, a body that is not hers in his mind, but his to 'smack', 'grab' and 'domesticate', as for him, there are no boundaries, only 'blurred lines'. Harmless fun. Just a joke. But who are the ones who are laughing? Not women.

George the Poet, in episode one of his podcast 'Have You Heard George's Podcast?', which opens with the sound of children's voices playing in the background, is direct in the questions he asks. 'Right now I'm Uncle George watching my nephews play with their friends'; he envisions what life might be like for them some twenty years on.

'Some of them will obviously be dead, some in jail, some sitting right here watching their own kids, asking the same questions.' He pauses, then continues. 'People get uncomfortable when you talk about children like that, like there's a cause and effect relationship between the things we say aloud and the way the future pans out. Like these negative prospects are less likely for our children if we don't acknowledge the current reality.' He ponders whether 'words' are powerful or whether they're just stories 'we tell ourselves to imagine power into existence'. He says that stories stay the same and nothing changes until 'the day you cross it out and replace it with a better answer'. Like Brown and Wittgenstein, Mpanga knows that words have power; to influence culture, to change behaviour, to impact lives. Words are political, words are like actions, words can enforce oppressive norms and scripts of dehumanisation just as much as they can inspire change, community, resilience and hope.

Love Story

This story is inspired by the experiences of survivors who have shared their stories with me and the testimonies submitted to Everyone's Invited.

Hey xx
Hi x
Hru? x
Gd thnks u? x
Wuu2? xxx
Nm just at home x
Wat u wearing? Have you ever watched porn? How far have you been? How many guys have you gw? Are you shaved? Can you add me on snap? Can you send me a pic? Do you watch porn? Wuu2 this weekend?

You've been talking every day for a few weeks now and you smile into the phone as it pings and it pings and he asks you if you're going out on the weekend and he invites you to a party at a house in London as the parents are away so you carefully choose your outfit that matches your eyeshadow and this is where you meet him and his friends who have the power and the keys to the world that they control and you make your way down the stairs into a large basement with big projectors and bottles of spirits and sticky walls and the girls who are dancing in jeans and crop tops with glossy lips and the boys at the back who are watching and sniggering and drinking and watching and there are no windows and the air is heavy and you feel the heat of the sweat and your cheeks are glowing as the vodka is coursing through your blood as your eyes are glazing over and you are trying to hold a conversation and music is blaring and suddenly you can feel his eyes on you staring right at you as if you are the only girl in the room and the only girl in the world and you understand for the first time in your life what it is to be seen and you think that this could be what real love is and he tells you that the quiet room upstairs is free and the parents aren't home and you've been plied with Smirnoff and Diet Coke and so you leave your girlfriends and the music and the noises behind to stumble up the stairs as you are being ushered forward by him and he is holding you up with his arm around your neck when he pulls you upstairs up into the quiet room and then your body is no longer yours as this boy has learnt from the screen and is doing what the screen has instructed him to do as he does things to you before you can agree and you've never done this before and you don't know how it's normally done and there's the banging at the door and the flashing lights and laughing voices in the background all whilst you are hurting but this is apparently how it goes as you are being crushed under the weight of a chest that is too heavy to push off and you are thinking of being elsewhere and drifting further and further away as your eyes are opening and closing and opening and closing and he is snapping his fingers in your face and asking you to stay awake and let him finish because he is almost almost almost almost there.

Ubiquitous Porn and Naïve Parents

Mine is the first generation to be born and raised in a digital age where there is no longer a distinction between the offline and the online, the 'real world' and the world of social media. Young people are coming of age in a world that is radically different to that of our parents. The way we communicate, the way we behave and interact, how we form relationships, engage with sexual partners and the way we consume news and information is divergently different from the generations before us. Bernardine Evaristo, in her novel *Girl, Woman, Other*, highlights this in her portrayal of the experience of Yazz, a university student who is a member of the 'Swipe-Like-Chat-Invite-Fuck Generation', where 'men expect you to give it up on the first (and only) date, have no pubic hair *at all*, and do disgusting things they've seen women do in porn movies on the internet which she suspects all the boys in her halls watch all day and all night'.[1] This is what it is to be a young person in the age of hardcore pornography, in the digital revolution of the social world, where anything goes. Ours is the first generation to be born and raised in a world where pornography is ubiquitous. Where porn is limitless and accessible to anyone, anytime and anywhere. Young people are coming into their own, developing as humans and finding identity through screens. And the screen is influential. Unlike anything that has existed before, galvanising millions of people on its platforms, and globalising information with extraordinary ease and accessibility. Our lives are being mediated, informed and rewired by the unchecked power of pornography and social media.

In the early days of Everyone's Invited, I was uncertain and apprehensive about taking a heavy stance on pornography. It is an area that felt controversial and fiercely contested, requiring that I tread cautiously. At the time, sex positivity felt like the better way forward, working against the shame and stigma associated with sex and by extension sexual violence. Sex positivity is a popular concept that has evolved in recent years, defined according to context. Broadly speaking, it is widely accepted that sex positivity is about supporting an openness to a variety of sexual orientations, interests (or lack thereof), identities and expressions. It is also understood as adopting a more joyful and positive approach to sex, which promotes the importance of pleasure and safety in relationships. Moreover, the adoption of a punitive stance or harsh legislation against the adult porn industry only puts the lives of sex workers (predominantly women and, in some cases, some of the most marginalised and vulnerable women) at increased risk. When you criminalise sex workers you push them further underground, forcing them to operate on the fringes of society, which means more stigma, more danger and fewer rights. Sex work has endured and thrived throughout every legal regime for centuries. Criminalisation or partial criminalisation has never, in practice, throughout history, successfully eliminated sex work.

So, what are the alternatives to adult porn? Is there a solution to the problems within and caused by the porn industry or a replacement for the current model? I thought about feminist porn and ethical porn, both of which exist today. Surely there's porn out there produced by people who champion loving, equal relationships and gender equality. Porn that celebrates sex and intimacy as a natural and healthy part of the human experience, where individuals can find meaningful connections, joy and love through sex. Erika Lust is an award-winning adult film-maker. As per her website, erikalust.com, Erika 'has been leading the revolution for adult cinema that goes beyond traditional gender roles and tired stereotypes'. Her films offer an alternative to mainstream porn in her commitment to representing a diverse variety of performers in body types, identities and sexualities. Lust is a proponent of the 'female gaze' and in all her productions she follows a set of principles that include focusing on female pleasure, promoting safe sex and ensuring all aspects of the film are agreed upon with the performers before a shoot begins. Her audiences have to buy her films to watch them unlike the bulk of mainstream porn available for free online. Whilst completing an internship at a marketing agency in London, I learnt about the app *Dipsea*, which is an audio 'story studio' featuring voice actors playing out sexy scenarios. The company's mission is to 'empower women to tap into sexuality more easily, and on their own terms'. *Dipsea* is also a subscription-based app that requires a monthly fee from their users. But who is actually consuming this kind of pornography? Is this something that's popular or widely watched amongst young people – or anyone for that matter? Porn that is produced to a high standard, with directors, actors, assistants and set designers who are treated fairly, and porn that resembles indie art-house cinema more than mainstream adult porn is *not* free of charge. Most people don't consider 'ethical pornography' as something worth spending their money on – why pay when porn is free and just a click away? Moreover, if you associate watching porn with shame and stigma, why pay for it and risk leaving evidence of your participation? Opening the incognito browser and typing the four letters into Google is the easiest, quickest and most discreet course of action.

In reality, ethical porn sites are not where the overwhelming majority of porn consumers are getting their porn. In a post-*Playboy* digital age, abuse, degradation, violence and the humiliation of individuals dominate the world's leading porn sites: XVideos, XNXX, Pornhub, xHamster, Realsrv, Stripchat, SpankBang, Chaturbate,

Jerkmate and BongaCams.[2] In 2019, Pornhub claimed they had forty-two billion visitors and thirty-nine billion searches performed.[3] With so much wide-ranging porn available at our fingertips, the content is more extreme than anything seen before, as distributers constantly push boundaries and exploit taboos to compete for their users' attention. In his book *The Brain that Changes Itself*, neuroscientist Dr Norman Doidge noted, 'Thirty years ago "hardcore" pornography usually meant the *explicit* depiction of sexual intercourse . . . Now hardcore has evolved and is increasingly dominated by the sadomasochistic themes . . . involving scripts fusing sex with hatred and humiliation.'[4]

Speaking to a friend about the impact of pornography on our lives, she told me about the first time she had seen it as a child. She was around eight years old and on a playdate when her friend showed her a porn clip on her parents' laptop. My friend described feeling scared and being scarred by the images as the memory of what she had seen was etched deep into her childhood brain, images she has never forgotten to this day. Around the age of eight or nine, I remember playing online games like *Club Penguin* – where you played games as a penguin avatar in a virtual world – and being bombarded with sexually explicit language in the open chat room. This was on a game that was targeted towards young children. As a young girl, my friends and I would join chat rooms like Omegle, where we would video-connect to strangers from around the world. Several of these rooms were filled with boys and young men who'd ask us to 'strip' or flash their dicks on the screen. When I asked a friend if she'd ever been on Omegle when she was younger, she said, 'Of course, everyone went on that. It was just a bunch of people wanking.' Back in the 2010s, before we had streaming services like Netflix, Disney+ and Amazon Prime, everyone would watch their favourite TV shows via pirated streaming websites. These links would spam our laptops with a slew of pop-up pornographic adverts, video cam girls and links to explicit content. When I first joined Facebook as a young teenager, I remember constantly being added as a friend and having to block much older creepy men who would bombard me with messages and unsolicited images. This still happens now on Instagram, as strangers can send images, messages and content via direct messages.

In an interview with Howard Stern on SiriusXM in December 2021, Billie Eilish discussed the impact of viewing pornography from a young age and throughout her teenage years. Having encountered it for the first time at eleven, she reports that the 'abusive' and 'brutal' scenes gave her nightmares, negatively affecting her understanding and expectations of what sex should look like. Eilish stated, 'I think porn is a disgrace. I used to watch a lot of porn, to be honest . . . I was an advocate and I thought I was one of the guys and would talk about it and think I was really cool for not having a problem with it and not seeing why it was bad.' She went on to say, 'I think it really destroyed my brain and I feel incredibly devastated that I was exposed to so much porn.'[5] Eilish encapsulates the confusing and conflicting view that many young people hold towards pornography consumption. There is pressure, curiosity, arousal, shock, shame, addiction, disgust and trauma. Pressure to be an 'advocate' is something I and many of my peers can relate to; a sense that speaking out against the industry makes you a 'prude' or old-fashioned amongst your peers. A reluctance to criticise pornography also comes from the very real anxiety that any fierce criticism of the industry might have a harmful impact on the lives and rights of sex workers who are in some cases already at risk and in vulnerable and precarious positions. As a teenager, being an advocate for pornography felt in line with the idea of 'sex positivity' in our approach to sex, sexuality and relationships. There is so much value in the promotion of pleasure and liberation in sex education. However, has sex positivity also become a guise that has allowed society to overlook abusive content, saturated as it is with grotesque racial tropes and extreme sexual violence?[6] Writing in *The Times* about Eilish's interview, journalist Janice Turner states that, 'Cancel culture has given porn a free pass.'[7]

Billie Eilish's refreshing honesty about watching porn as a young person is affirming. All young people have watched porn but fear sharing these experiences with adults who they worry will respond with judgement and hostility rather than help and support. Eilish acknowledges that porn made her 'not say no to things that were not good' when she first began having sex because 'I thought that's what I was supposed to be attracted to'. Eilish is probably alluding to the extreme expectations of sex that hardcore pornography presents and condones. The rise in popularity and mainstreaming of hardcore, body-punishing, sadomasochistic pornography has reshaped the sex lives of my generation, training the brain to associate violence with pleasure. What is viewed and consumed online is being translated into real sex lives, with the growing expectation of women to participate in degrading sex acts. Bryant Paul, a professor of telecommunications at Indiana University Bloomington, whose work is centred around script theory (a psychological theory contending that human behaviour conforms to patterns called 'scripts'), made the claim that adults would be 'foolish' to not think that young people are getting ideas about sex from porn. Arguing that repeated exposure to certain themes would lead to an internalisation of these sexual scripts.[8] Pornographic sexual scripts depict men as aggressive and controlling and women as submissive and sexually objectified.[9] Moreover, Pornhub's 2021 'Year in Review' saw the popularity of the 'How To' search skyrocket by 244 per cent. The search option has over 200,000 videos with some of the most popular tags including how to 'eat pussy', 'suck dick', 'put on a condom', 'last longer', 'finger myself', 'find g spot', and 'how to make her cum'.[10] A recent survey of more than a thousand undergraduate students found that a third said that they 'learned more about sex from pornography than from formal education'.[11] Where there is little accessible and comprehensive sex education available, porn is the medium through which young people are learning how to have sex.

Commenting in *The Times* in 2018, activist and writer Laura Bates – founder of the Everyday Sexism Project – said that porn made teenage boys believe that making girls cry was just 'part of foreplay'. Bates shares her experience of visiting a school and the conversations she had with young pupils about pornography.

> I went to a school recently where they had a rape case involving a 14-year-old boy and a teacher had said to him, 'Why didn't you stop when she was crying?' and he looked straight back at her quite bewildered and said, 'Because it is normal for girls to cry during sex.' . . . I go into schools and talk to children around that age all the time who think that crying is part of foreplay because they have seen so much online porn that normalises violence and treats women in a way that is incredibly misogynistic and dehumanising.[12]

Young people believe that porn is real. Thirteen-year-old girls are on TikTok making jokes about being slapped, choked and spat on during sex. Fiona Mackenzie founded the campaign group We Can't Consent To This after noticing a rise in the number of cases where consent is used as a defence in so-called 'sex games gone wrong'. She is exposing how women are being murdered at the hands of their sexual partners. Speaking to the BBC in 2019, she said, 'I regularly hear from women who had been choked, slapped, spat on, verbally abused and punched by men they were having otherwise consensual sex with. In many cases, women weren't initially able to recognise this as the traumatic assault it is.'[13] We Can't Consent To This has documented the deaths of fifty-nine women in the UK where 'sex game gone wrong' has been cited as cause of death.[14] A 2019 survey of 2,002 UK women aged eighteen to thirty-nine found that more than a third had experienced slapping, choking, gagging or spitting during consensual sex and that they were unwanted 'at least some of the time'.[15] The research came in the wake of the murder of British backpacker Grace Millane which gained international attention as the case heard the defence of 'rough sex' being utilised in court. Writer Briony Smith concluded in an investigative report for *Flare* that, 'Choking, it seems, has become the new third base.'[16]

Many of the testimonies that we have received on Everyone's Invited reflect these experiences as the sex lives of young people are becoming more 'pornified', male-centric and aggressive with an absence of focus on female pleasure. When I first began sharing the testimonies of my peers in June 2020, I received one account describing an experience of being suddenly penetrated anally with violence and force midway through sex, without consent. After being posted, I then received another with the comment, 'omg this happened to me too', and then another and another, and another, and another. A study of 4,009 heterosexual scenes from two major pornographic tube sites (Pornhub and XVideos) found that women were the target of aggression in 97 per cent of scenes.[17]

There is nothing more influential than the consumption of pornography on a young person's understanding and conception of what sex is and what it should look like. In May 2021, my team and I engaged in a series of conversations with parents whose children were victims of rape in primary school who have been lobbying the Department for Education and Ofsted for many years. In 2018, accounts and calls to action from the parents were published in *The Times Educational Supplement*, which detailed the harrowing reality child victims face in the aftermath of assault: they are subjected to intimidating police interviews, and have their bodies photographed and scraped for evidence, then are left with little to no support from social services and are faced with six- to eighteen-month-long waiting lists for counselling. It was then revealed that the young boys were routinely watching hardcore pornography on their parents' laptops. According to police figures in England and Wales, on average one child is raped in school on every school day, and in primary schools alone three sexual assaults are reported to the police every school day.[18]

• • •

Porn is a performance. There are actors, there are porn stars, there are directors, there are camera operators. Those who are doing the performing are paid for this performance.

We know that it's not real, we know that it's performative and we know that it is fantasy. Yet, according to philosopher and academic Amia Srinivasan, we are witnessing the unravelling of this truth. The truth is being inverted as real-life sex becomes closer to the porn we see onscreen. Srinivasan's conversations with her university students about the impact of pornography on their lives convey this same message: porn is reshaping the sex lives of those who consume it. Her students' responses confirmed her fears that porn doesn't merely depict but enacts the subordination of women; that it silences women and makes it harder for them to speak out and protest against unwanted sex, that it is responsible for the objectification of women, the marginalisation of women, as well as sanctioning real violence against women. She writes that 'sex for my students is what porn says it is',[19] that it presents them with a fully formed and interpreted sexual script that dictated their real sex lives – the moves, gestures, physical demands, sounds, desires as well as the appropriate distributions of power. She observes that the 'psyches of the students are the products of pornography'.[20]

This 'pornographic script' is determining the sex lives of those who are exposed to it, both directly and indirectly via their partners. On the screen, there is violence. Rape fantasies, incest, paedophilia, real sexual violence – are all condoned, normalised and encouraged. A caricatured depiction of female pleasure can trump any authentic portrayal of female pleasure in the pornographic script.

There is a 'significant overall relationship between

pornography consumption and attitudes supporting violence against women' according to a 2010 meta-analysis.[21] Regular consumers are also more likely to report an intent to rape[22] and to commit sexual assault,[23] and less likely to empathise with rape victims.[24] Meanwhile, in one study of sorority members, the women who watched porn were less likely to intervene when they saw other women being sexually assaulted.[25] Studies have shown that regular consumers of porn are less likely to support affirmative action for women,[26] and that regular teenage boy consumers were much more likely to view girls as 'playthings' and perceive sex as a purely physical act. This rings true for my own teenage sexual experiences and that of my peers, and is affirmed in the testimonies. Sex for young people, especially teenagers, is often devoid of intimacy, connection or love. For teenagers, it has evolved into more of a casual and unequal physical exchange, part of the rise of 'hook-up culture', which advocates emotionless no-strings sex. A culture where girls 'give' sexual pleasure but rarely receive, whilst boys fuck with ambivalence and detachment, porno style. Sex is a badge of honour for the boy – racking up the numbers is a way to attain social clout – but sex is also the mark of 'slut' on a girl. No sex, however, is even worse, where the label of 'virgin' or 'frigid' is swiftly applied.

In her essay 'Talking to My Students About Porn', Srinivasan highlights how the anti-porn feminists of the 1970s and 1980s fervently communicated their warnings about pornography. She cites the work of Andrea Dworkin,

Robin Morgan and Catharine MacKinnon to drive her point home. Though porn at the time felt marginal – a glimpse here and magazine there, a stolen trip to the cinema in the early hours of the morning – anti-porn campaigners theorised 'pornography as a virtual training ground for male violence and aggression'.[27] In its production and consumption, the pornography industry bears direct responsibility for inciting violence against women in its eroticising and sanctioning of humiliation, abuse and dehumanisation of female bodies, as argued by Andrea Dworkin in *Pornography: Men Possessing Women* (1981). In 1974, feminist radical and activist Robin Morgan reinforced this idea in her declaration that, 'Pornography is the theory, and rape is the practice.' Anti-porn feminist and campaigner Catharine MacKinnon prophesied a disturbing vision of the future, imagining the long-term implications of a society raised on widespread pornography consumption. The image she paints feels ever more urgent in the context of how pornography has evolved in recent years. Writing in *Only Words,* MacKinnon reminds us of the different dimensions in which consumers live out pornography, from teachers who are unable to view female students as equals to doctors who may molest anaesthetised women.[28] There are men in the criminal justice system, from serving on juries to answering police calls, who report domestic violence. There are directors and producers making mainstream films. There are men who sexually harass their employees and clients, or molest daughters and beat their wives, and college students who gang rape women in fraternities. 'Some become serial rapists and sex murderers – using and making pornography is inextricable in these acts.'[29]

The image she creates is frightening yet eerily familiar to the reality of our time. MacKinnon depicts a society where the impact of porn can be felt in almost every aspect of life, in a world where everyone has consumed or is regularly consuming pornography. What is viewed on the screen is transmogrified into everyday interactions, in professional and educational environments, permeating both the private and the public spheres and influencing our day-to-day lives. Those who will assume key positions of power in every industry, those who influence the lives of millions will inevitably, in a world where pornography is ubiquitous, be influenced in their actions, behaviour and decision-making by what they have consumed on the screen.

Today, most young people will be exposed to hardcore pornography before they have received access to any form of sex education. The lives of young people have become incomprehensible to their parents. This division, this growing sense of polarisation between the young and the old, is inhibiting our collective ability to find solutions to the problems we now face. More than ever, we need to choose to listen to each other, as never before has there been a greater gap between the lived experiences of the young and those of the old. Many parents have overlooked the responsibility and necessity in educating and preparing their children to grow up in a digital world where much of life now exists in the virtual sphere.

Since the launch of Everyone's Invited, we have heard complaints from parents who accuse the platform of threatening the innocence of their children by the publication of testimonies about sexual violence. Such a response is indicative of extreme naïvety and the wild disconnect of some adults in our digital age. The older generation must face up to the reality of the world that we live in. It is critical that we engage openly in these conversations with one another, that parents cultivate environments at home free from judgement and shame where their children feel safe and able to share their online experiences. The same can be said in what is and what is still not being covered in the Relationships and Sex Education curriculum in schools. At my secondary school, it felt like we watched the same video in ICT (Information and Communication Technology) class every year, depicting a young girl being groomed online by a forty-year-old man who pressures her to send him naked images in the bath. Whilst grooming is a problem that young people face, this singular and narrow representation of online sexual abuse by no means even began to encompass the ever growing and ever changing diversity of abusive behaviours that we were experiencing on the internet and on social media throughout our teenage years. Education in and around pornography did not exist. We need even more comprehensive, better informed and more engaging sex education. Sex education that's delivered by specialists or well-trained teachers who are confident and comfortable with the material. Sex education that's taken seriously. Sex education that tells young people that porn isn't real life, that sex should not be inextricable from violence, that women are not objects, that girls don't have to emulate the degrading, dehumanising acts that are ubiquitous online. That girls' pleasure in sex matters too. Sex education that's inclusive, non-judgemental and empathetic. Sex education that's designed to empower young people to develop loving, healthy, respectful, pleasurable and equal intimate relationships.

The Collectors

Teenage courtship begins online. For young people, the real world and the virtual world are intertwined – boys and girls are increasingly living out their lives within the digital sphere. As sexual abuse and harassment exist in the real world, it will inevitably permeate the virtual. Patriarchal gender norms such as the belief that men are entitled to sex, the idea that men have an uncontrollable sexual appetite, the notion that sex is a form of achievement, and that women are objects with transactional value to be rated, shared and shamed both inform and influence the growing prevalence of abuse that has manifested in the digital world.[1] In many ways, we have seen an acceleration of abusive behaviours in the age of hardcore pornography and social media, yet social media is, like many things, a double-edged sword. It is also a force for positive social change and activism. It has mobilised and empowered social movements across the globe by making access to information easier and facilitating platforms where communities can grow.

Everyone's Invited was built on the platforms of social media, gaining momentum through sharing and resharing information and stories on Instagram, Twitter and TikTok. We have gone viral multiple times on multiple platforms, where we have successfully captured the attention of and started conversations on these issues with millions of people. The testimonies themselves can be read on our website, which can be accessed by anyone, anytime, from any country in the world.

But social media platforms have also directly enabled and exacerbated age-old abuses and harmful behaviours online. My grandmother's street flasher is now a thirteen-year-old's unsolicited dick pic on Snapchat. The derogatory 'get back in the kitchen' remark at a dinner party is now an Instagram meme. Old-fashioned misogyny has morphed into toxic online subcultures, lurking in the depths of Reddit and Facebook.[2] These groups strategically work to radicalise boys and young men, indoctrinating them in supremacist and anti-feminist ideologies, which are steadily seeping into the mainstream. A new spectrum of behaviours and types of abuse has manifested online, emerging in the past ten years and growing with extreme prevalence amongst young people who spend more and more of their lives fixated on these platforms. In December 2021, I was invited to join a panel discussion to launch a groundbreaking report titled 'Understanding and Combatting Youth Experiences of Image-Based Sexual Harassment and Abuse', published by academics from University College London, the University of Kent and the University of Leicester (hereafter referred to as the UCL report). It was a virtual session and key stakeholders who I had become acquainted with over the previous year through my work were in attendance. These included Professor Jessica Ringrose, Dr Kaitlyn Regehr and Betsy Milne, who co-authored the report.[3] The report itself aims 'to shift how young people, schools and parents' identify and respond to image-based sexual harassment and abuse. It was a highly informative and engaging event with groundbreaking, nuanced and critical insights from experts within the field. Professor Jessica Ringrose announced that, 'We are in the midst of a crisis of digital sexual violence in the UK at present,' and called for 'proactive solutions over reactive ones'. Academics use the terms 'image-based sexual harassment' and 'image-based abuse' to define these new behaviours.

1. Image-based sexual harassment (IBSH) describes two forms of digital sexual violence, which are:
   1.1. unwanted sexual images, for example, cyber flashing or unsolicited dick pics, and
   1.2. unwanted solicitation for sexual images.[4]
2. Image-based sexual abuse (IBSA) refers to the non-consensual recording, distribution and/or threat of distribution of nude or sexual images. Although sometimes referred to as 'revenge porn' in popular culture, this term fails to account for the many different contexts in which IBSA can take place.

As is described in the report, these new forms of abuse are heavily influenced by gender norms and overwhelmingly target and negatively impact the lives of young girls. Platforms like Snapchat and Instagram facilitate and enable image-based harassment and abuse and create opportunities for perpetrators – most frequently known and unknown teenage boys and adult men – to access and harass both known and unknown people. On Snapchat, quick adds, snap streaks, snap scores and the lack of identity verification seamlessly enable the prevalence of image-based harassment and abuse on young people's phones. On Instagram, the direct messages and group chat function facilitate unwanted sexual content and contact.[5] Throughout my teenage years, and even to this day, I am still randomly added to porn bot sex chats that bombard explicit content to random users. According to the findings of the UCL report, image-based sexual harassment overwhelmingly impacts girls: 75 per cent of girls received dick pics, 37 per cent of girls compared to 20 per cent of boys reported receiving unwanted sexual content, and upon receiving unwanted sexual content 80 per cent of girls reported feeling 'disgusted' and 58 per cent felt 'confused'.[6]

The UCL report also stresses the necessity of an inter-sectional approach to contextualised harm as, 'IBSA risk and harms are not simply gendered but, also, deeply classed and raced, with young people having variable access to support. Thus, we argue for a nuanced approach to under-standing and contextualising digital sexual violence.' The findings emphasised the deeply gendered nature of this form of abuse as 'boys were rewarded for sharing girls' images amongst their peers, as an indication of their masculinity status', whilst 'girls were shamed and victim-blamed for having their image shared without their consent'.[7] The report found that nudes held transactional value and those boys who engaged in their collection achieved social status and currency. Furthermore, it found that some images held higher value than others, for example, images that had never been seen by groups were the most coveted. The higher the level of trust violation, the more the boys are validated socially and rewarded by their peers. More disturbingly, boys who attended schools that offered media literacy education and who were aware of the perceived risk associated with trading images adapted their behaviour to avoid detection and minimise risk. Instead of sending content that leaves a digital footprint, they showed their peers the images on their screens in person, so that there was no evidence of image sharing. Throughout my teenage years, I distinctly remember this happening amongst some of the boys I socialised with. They openly showed nudes of girls that they had on their phones to groups of friends at pubs and house parties. With the increasing prevalence of this specific form of image-based abuse, there is a growing phenomenon of hidden victimisation as many young women and girls are likely to unknowingly be victims of this form of digital violence. Inundated with unwanted explicit content regularly, the result is a normalisation of this form of harassment for young people as they do not think of these activities as harassment. Conversations conducted with schoolgirls in the UCL report clearly demonstrate a widespread acceptance of these behaviours amongst young people. One girl shared that it was so common that 'it's not shocking anymore, you just get on with your life', and another said that you just 'laugh and then you carry on'. Other girls told the interviewers that they didn't think it was a big deal because 'it happens to everyone'.[8]

Rather than viewing these incidents as a form of digital sexual violence, young people are perceiving them as a tiring phenomenon that is 'just a part of life'. Amongst my peers growing up, as is also revealed in the UCL report, humour is often used as a way of coping and dealing with these violations, though humour serves to both normalise and trivialise this pervasive form of online sexual abuse. In line with the 2021 Ofsted report's findings[9] (commissioned in response to Everyone's Invited), the UCL report also found that these forms of image-based harassment and abuse are being experienced on a daily basis and have become part and parcel of young people's lives. Having visited thirty-two schools and spoken to nine hundred children and young people, Ofsted reported that, '90 per cent of girls, and nearly 50 per cent of boys, said being sent explicit pictures or videos of things they did not want to see happens a lot or sometimes to them or their peers'. Moreover, Ofsted found that the amassing of 'nudes' has been likened to a 'collection game' for young boys. The testimonies and the findings of the UCL and Ofsted reports all show young people viewing these experiences as unremarkable. Young girls have repeatedly described a process of 'getting used to it', viewing it as 'not serious enough to report' because it 'happens all the time'. One of the key findings of the UCL report was that young people rarely report incidents of image-based sexual harassment and abuse. It states that 'rates of reporting to either the social media platforms or to parents or school were nearly non-existent'. Ofsted highlighted the many barriers victims face in reporting these experiences of sexual harassment and violence. These included:

worry that what happened next would be out of their control; worry that they would be branded by their peers as a 'snitch' who got their peer in trouble; worry that they would be ostracised from friendship groups; worry that there would be damage to their reputation, for example through sexual rumours being circulated about them; feeling that they would not be believed; feeling that they might be blamed for doing things they were told not to do, for example sending nudes, even if they were pressured to do so; feeling that nothing would be done; feeling that things were so commonplace 'there's no point' in raising it; feeling embarrassment and shame when talking to someone from a different generation about sex.[10]

The stigma and shame associated with these experiences and the resulting difficulties victims face in seeking support or reporting incidents were also seen in the testimonies on

Everyone's Invited. At school, 'nudes' were sent around like 'wildfire'. Some testimonies detailed experiences of girls – some as young as twelve – being coerced into sending nudes through an incessant barrage of manipulative messages from older or 'cooler' boys who held more power and social clout. In one case, the girl had been brave enough to report this coercion to a member of staff at her school. But instead of being met with support, she faced shame and punishment as she was suspended from school whilst her perpetrator went unpunished. Her images – images of a *child* – were shared amongst her peers without her consent, and she was bullied, laughed at, shamed, humiliated and ostracised at school by both the boys and the girls. Some testimonies told harrowing stories of boys hosting intimate images of underage girls on Google Drive and WhatsApp groups, which could be accessed by hundreds of boys across London. One submission revealed how one girl had been permanently scarred for life after, as a teenager, her 'nudes' had been projected onto the walls of a house party full of teenagers. She was told the next day that 'her nudes were up' and was branded a 'slut' by her peers. Those who refused to participate would be shamed as 'frigid' and would all too often bow to the pressure after relentless manipulative messages from boys who held social power and clout. One entry described how a girl was pressured by a boy with whom she had never had more than two minutes' face-to-face conversation at school. They insisted that it was 'normal', 'what everyone does', and it would be 'boring if they didn't'. In some cases these images were then used as a tool of power and humiliation by the 'popular' boys, boasting about how they would masturbate over them and rating them with their friends on group chats on WhatsApp and Facebook messenger.

Even more harrowingly were the stories that detailed post-separation abuse, where ex-partners would use the possession of such images to control and blackmail their ex. Many of the testimonies describe the pressure girls faced from their boyfriends to be filmed whilst they were engaging in sexual acts. One entry recounted a disturbing experience of a teenage girl who found hundreds of images and videos on her boyfriend's laptop of her naked body that had been taken whilst she was sleeping or had been secretly filmed without her knowledge during sex.

Digital violence was equally rife on university campuses, as some testimonies recounted distressing stories about the degrading antics and misogynistic lad culture of sports teams. One testimony described how the rugby team engaged in a tradition that involved getting the girls they were sleeping with to wear their rugby shirts and take pictures from behind 'doggy style' and share them on their rugby Facebook chat. The images and videos would be rated, shared, and laughed at as girl's bodies and sexual 'abilities' were ranked on a scale of one to ten. The stories shared in the testimonies powerfully highlight the multi-layered and complex nature of digital violence, as power is abused and reinforced as images are used as a tool to coerce, control, humiliate, silence and oppress.

In recent years, tech and social media companies have come under increasing pressure to regulate and implement action to reduce the abuse thriving on their platforms. In December 2021, major changes were proposed in the UK's landmark Online Safety Bill, which seeks to regulate tech giants and social media. Chairman of the joint committee on the draft bill, Damian Collins, said, 'What's illegal offline should be regulated online. For too long, big tech has gotten away with being the land of the lawless . . . The era of self-regulation for big tech has come to an end.' The three main objectives of the draft Online Safety Bill are to 'Tackle illegal content and activity', 'Protect children', and 'Give adults greater control, while protecting freedom of expression'.[11] Some of the key recommendations include an 'explicit duty for all pornography sites to make sure children cannot access them', that it is not only content that should be targeted but the potentially harmful impact of algorithms.[12] Collins went on to claim that the changes would 'bring more offences clearly within the scope of the Online Safety Bill, give Ofcom the power in law to set minimum safety standards for the services they will regulate, and to take enforcement action against companies if they don't comply'.[13] Yet some have criticised this bill on grounds of free speech.

So how do we begin to address a problem so vast, so pervasive and so normalised amongst a generation of young people? I will return to Jessica Ringrose's suggestion that these solutions must be proactive rather than reactive. We need to begin this education early in our children's lives, starting with conversations around safety and technology. Even if your child does not possess a smartphone, it is likely that they will find access to an electronic device via another family member, friend or peer. Developing in young people an understanding of the different forms of online abuse is crucial and this begins with building literacy; children need a comprehensive education in what constitutes image-based abuse and harassment, and the different forms these can take, so they are able to identify and communicate with confidence if they experience something abusive online. We must be informed, non-judgemental and empathetic in our approach. Solutions must come from every level of society, involving young people, parents, carers, teachers, tech companies, child welfare professionals and government.

If we are to make sense of this new reality and find solutions to these increasingly complex problems, we must bridge these generational gaps. We need to be able to understand each other and listen to each other's experiences. The victim-blaming mentality is prevalent amongst older generations who narrowly assume that this form of abuse can be stopped if we simply tell young girls to stop sending nudes. What must be understood by parents, teachers and the older generations alike is that the digital world and 'real' world are intrinsically intertwined for young people. All parents today must understand that digital communication is an inextricable part of children's and teenagers' lives. The division between the online and offline worlds that might still exist in parents' lives does not exist in the lives of today's children. Young people build connections online, they form friendships, romantic relationships, develop their own identity, and make sense of the world around them on the internet and on social media. 'Digital sex' – the consensual sending of nudes and sexting – is 'real sex' for a generation that has come of age in the digital social world. The implication is that adults need to start reframing the way they respond and speak to young people. Approaching these issues with an attitude of judgement or shame will only foster an isolating environment for children where they will not have the confidence to share their experiences, go to parents for help if needed, or seek parental support if they have experienced any form of digital violence. The UCL report recommends that parents should 'avoid taking an overly negative and disciplinary approach to your child's technology use'.

Research shows that children often avoid telling their parents about their experiences of sexual harassment and abuse because they worry about being punished or having their technology taken away. Crucially, children must feel that if they experience online abuse, they will not be in trouble if they confide in an adult.[14]

Parents need to talk to their children and cultivate an environment at home where children feel comfortable and able to share their online experiences. Talk about 'nudes', talk openly about pornography in a non-judgemental space. It's important for parents to be supportive and begin cultivating an honest and trusting relationship around social media and mobile phone use rather than imposing strict rules and focusing all efforts on restricting or outright banning devices. In this setting, young people will feel more able to share their experiences and communicate incidents that have made them feel weird, upset, uncomfortable or angry. Open and honest communication will allow parents more opportunities to educate and raise awareness around different forms of image-based abuse that they might face as a young person. If a child or teenager has been a victim of digital violence, they will feel much more comfortable in not only disclosing their experience but also seeking help with the support of a parent.

There is no obvious answer to this multi-layered problem. If technology and social media are here to stay then we need to be doing more to protect each other online. Everyone deserves to be safe online, especially young people, who are the most vulnerable and the most impressionable. Education is essential and regulation is important. Openness, empathy and enduring communication is needed if we are to meaningfully tackle these issues together.

Nothing Compares
to an English Rose

My friend, who is also half Chinese, told me a story that has always stayed with me. She had gone on holiday with a white school friend and her friend's family, who had also invited some of their own adult friends. She was having dinner with everyone one night, including her friend's brother. He was on a gap year and had recently been travelling in South East Asia. As the meal wore on, a family friend asked the brother about his travels. 'Where did you go? How was the food? But most importantly, how were the women?' He laughed and added, 'But of course, nothing compares to an English rose.' Shocked, my friend looked around the table. The guests were laughing, eating and chattering away. No one seemed to take any notice of this racially charged comment that played into a racist stereotype that hypersexualises Asian women whilst implying that white women, the 'English roses', were, without a doubt, infinitely more desirable. She was stunned and speechless, tears began to fill her eyes. Later in the evening, she

145

confronted her friend who responded with genuine surprise and confusion – she didn't understand why she was upset. At the time my friend thought to herself, *Did she really not hear what he said? Or did she just not register why this comment was so dehumanising and offensive?*

Having grown up with some white friends who accepted me as 'one of their own', not like the other Asians but a 'cool Asian', I viewed myself to be 'hot for an Asian' or a 'pretty Asian'. As a teenager, I never really felt beautiful and was not considered 'girlfriend material' amongst my group of mostly white peers. My white female friends – especially the blonde ones – who were conventionally attractive, always had boyfriends and were the most desired in the group. My Black female friends, who despite being very beautiful, were also made to feel undesirable in the white-dominated environments they navigated at school and university. They struggled to find boyfriends who would take them seriously and when they did, they often found themselves the object of a fetish, discovering that Blackness was the common denominator in a string of ex-girlfriends. Around the age of sixteen, I distinctly remember a white boy bragging about how he'd managed to get with the only Black girl on his summer course, boasting that he could finally 'tick it off his bucket list'.

'I'm not racist, I'm just not attracted to Black girls', 'Asians aren't my type', 'I don't like Asian men', 'I only date Asian women', 'Brown girls are my type'. Despite what so many may believe, these are not assertions of 'preference', they are manifestations of sexual racism; discrimination in romantic selection or sexual preference on the basis of perceived racial identity. Sexual racism, in short, can be understood as the use of racial stereotypes to either exclude or fetishise specific racial groups. Exclusion and fetishisation can be viewed as two extremes on opposite ends of the spectrum of sexual racism. Fetishisation can be an equally debilitating and dehumanising experience. Black and Asian minority groups are profoundly affected by such stereotypes, an experience all too common in my own life and those of my non-white peers.

I remember the feelings of shame and humiliation provoked by the frequent intersection of sexism and racism, a double oppression that I experienced for the first time in my early teenage years. Walking down the streets of London as a young girl and being leered at by a group of older men is a frightening experience, but to be accosted with racialised slurs like 'Chinese pussy' and 'tight Asian vagina' imposes another, more disturbing, layer of dehumanisation. I don't think I've ever been to a club or a party where white boys haven't cornered me and insisted that I tell them where I'm 'from from'. That is, they want to know where my parents are from so they can establish what my race is because they can see I'm not white – I'm something else, something 'exotic'. At around the age of seventeen, I remember a boy showing me an image on his iPhone of a Japanese porn star, posing in a tiny thong, with her back arched and breasts exposed. 'You look just like her – you look exactly like Asa Akira.' This was not the first or the last time I would elicit the comparison with this particular Japanese porn star. Throughout my time at school and university, multiple white boys who I encountered at parties, on nights out, in halls and in class told me about their 'Asian fetishes' and 'yellow fever', and about how they exclusively watched Asian or 'hentai' porn. In my early teenage years, the attention made me feel special and somehow validated, as if I was cooler or sexier than the other girls. As if I was finally being noticed, and finally being seen as 'desirable' and 'attractive', especially in a white environment where I had long felt excluded and written off almost immediately by some white boys.

Yet this type of dehumanisation is no compliment. Being reduced to a fetish is a demeaning and traumatic experience; an experience that many people of colour and minority individuals are forced to endure in white-dominated spaces. Reducing human beings to arbitrary labels or categories, as overtly seen in the categories of porn, such as Asian, ebony and Latina, is infinitely degrading and reductive. Sociologist Katherine Cross wrote, 'To some white men, Asian women top their hierarchies of desirability. But what do these women get out of that? Suffocating stereotypes of docility; discrimination; abuse. These are the wages of being in someone *else's* hierarchy.'[1] This hierarchy is a white man's hierarchy, a pecking order of women sorted by race, organised as objects in a pyramid of racialised desire. Historically, stereotypes formed around particular cultural, racial and ethnic identities reduce living and breathing multifaceted individuals to lifeless caricatures. Asian women are portrayed as submissive, obedient and 'exotic'; Latinas are 'feisty, wild and easily available'; and Black women are immune to pain and hypersexualised. Amia Srinivasan talks about 'fuckability' and 'unfuckability', referring not to innate sexual desire but to a racialised hierarchy constructed by Western sexual politics that places white women at the apex of desirability, Asian women beneath them, and Black and brown women ranking below them. 'Fuckability,' she writes, 'is precisely the product of the "differences in how society rewards you for fucking blondes v black women".'[2] A blonde or an 'English rose' is the most coveted woman in Western society and the Asian woman, whilst supremely 'fuckable', is not 'wifeable'. Even as a person of colour, your place on this hierarchy is inherently defined by your proximity to Eurocentric beauty standards. My experiences of degrading fetishising and sexual racism as a half Chinese woman have been less extreme than those of my full Asian peers who have navigated the same white, Western environments. It is crucial to recognise how, in a white environment, we have already been preconditioned to find white faces more attractive as consumers of a white-dominated media and popular culture. Beauty standards, attraction and desire are not internal manifestations but external impositions, an insidious conditioning of our subconscious.

Over the past year, I conducted a series of interviews with Evie Muir, a domestic abuse specialist and former frontline domestic violence support worker, who agreed to share some of her experiences as both a Black survivor of sexual violence and a domestic abuse specialist who has worked for a number of organisations across the violence against women and girls (VAWG) sector. Evie is from the north of England and she runs a walking club for survivors in the Peak District in her free time. She is kind, open and easy to talk to. She spoke candidly about her experiences at length, which is rare in my experience of engaging with survivors, who often struggle to articulate beyond the layers of trauma and pain. She talked freely but with a notable heaviness. As we began our conversation, over a shaky internet connection on FaceTime, I felt her disillusionment, as if she almost couldn't believe that she was still working in the field that has repeatedly re-traumatised and isolated her. 'The violence against women and girls sector is itself violent,' she tells me, relaying the institutional racism, transphobia, Islamophobia, and wider bias she's witnessed in the sector. Despite it all, she said, 'I just don't know how I can do anything else.' She told me that all of her encounters with violence, from street harassment to intimate partner violence, have been marked by sexual racism and racialised misogyny. As a child, she witnessed her African Caribbean father abuse her white mother. Racialised sexual violence has been present in all her relationships, from her first in secondary school all the way to university. Evie was fetishised and overly sexualised as a dual heritage Black woman by her partners who'd tell her they 'only liked Black girls'.

In her relationships she's experienced physical, psychological, and sexual violence, and was silenced and manipulated by her partners who exploited the ways that growing up Black instils a level of vulnerability and an instinctive fear of the police. Her white partners would say things like, 'Your skin doesn't bruise in the same way as white women, so the police will never believe you' and, 'I know you'll never go to the police because you don't trust them.' When she did eventually go to the police, an officer gave her abuser a warning, and told her, 'You shouldn't have any more trouble, he seems like an alright guy – I'm a good judge of character.' As the abuse escalated into post-separation abuse, her partner manipulated the institutional racism of the police and mental health systems to their advantage, exploiting racial stereotypes by painting her as the 'crazy Black woman' and positioning themselves as the 'caring white partner'. The gaslighting which underpinned this relationship led to her being institutionalised for two weeks in a mental health facility. Despite repeated disclosures, the staff never identified or recorded domestic abuse as a safeguarding concern, and she was released into her abuser's care with the highly politicised mental health diagnosis of borderline personality disorder, which he would later weaponise as a tool of further abuse.

Not only are Black women statistically more likely to experience domestic abuse and sexual violence, they are systematically failed by institutions that exist to help them, whether that be the criminal justice system, the police, mental health services or charities in the VAWG sector.

Implicit racial bias, ignorance and systemic racism create hostile environments for survivors of African and Caribbean heritage, where their needs are ignored, overlooked, and they are too often re-traumatised in the places tasked with supporting their healing and recovery. The Office for National Statistics found that adults of Black, Black British and mixed ethnicity were more likely to experience sexual assault than those of white, Asian or any other ethnicity. According to the Institute for Women's Policy Research in the US, more than 20 per cent of Black women have been victims of rape. 'In adulthood, approximately 1 in 5 African American women reported that they had been raped at some point in their lifetime . . . The National Intimate Partner and Sexual Violence Survey revealed that 41% of Black women experienced sexual coercion and other forms of unwanted sexual contact. These prevalent rates translate to an estimated 3.1 million Black survivors of other forms of sexual violence.'[3]

• • •

In December 2021, I attended a fundraiser in support of Sistah Space: 'a community-based non-profit initiative created to bridge the gap in domestic abuse services for African heritage women and girls'. The event's atmosphere was one of community and support, a genuine safe space for survivors of colour and those working in the violence against women sector. I was moved by the speakers on the panel who shared their experiences as Black women navigating the sector, the many barriers and abuses that they have faced over the years. They spoke about 'burnout', racism at work and the power of speaking their truth in a white-dominated sector that can be both hostile and abusive for workers and survivors of colour. Sistah Space offers advocacy, advice, emotional and practical support for survivors of African and Caribbean heritage. It was founded on the understanding that Black survivors see the highest rates of under-reporting, and that 86 per cent of African and/or Caribbean heritage women in the UK have either been a victim of domestic violence or sexual abuse, or know a family member who has been assaulted.

The charity came into existence in the wake of the passing of Valerie Forde and her twenty-two-month-old daughter, Jahzara. On 31 March 2014, they were murdered at the family home in London by Valerie's former partner Roland McKoy. Six weeks prior to her murder, despite Valerie's reports to the police, McKoy's threats to burn the house down with her in it were recorded as a 'threat to property' by officers. For this community, Valerie's murder highlighted the injustice that Black survivors of domestic abuse face in both the violence they experience and the failures of institutional systems in place to adequately support them and keep them safe from such violence. Valerie's murder was the catalyst for the formation of Sistah Space and their campaign, Valerie's Law, which calls for 'cultural competency training' for all institutions dealing with Black survivors to educate government agencies, practitioners, support workers and police officers. It will equip people with a comprehensive understanding of the unique experiences of African and Caribbean heritage survivors, accounting for the array of cultural nuances, barriers, colloquialisms, languages and customs that make up the diverse Black community.[4] Speaking to the *Guardian* in September 2021, Sistah Space chief executive Ngozi Fulani asserted that:

> Without mandating this life-saving training, black women are left to gamble with their lives on whether the officer responding to the scene is able to spot the unique signs of abuse in black environments on black skin. Too often black women are failed by law enforcement, paying with their lives for mistakes that can be avoided by simply implementing Valerie's Law . . . There is a lack of trust because the police are not taking black women who have been assaulted seriously. They are not always believed and there is a pervasive stereotype of black women being tough and not as in need of protection as white women. A lot of our service users are returning to abusive situations, are giving up or are even suicidal.[5]

Fear and distrust of the police, police brutality and institutional racism prevent Black survivors from reporting their experiences, seeking support and justice as they fear for the safety of their abusers in the hands of a police system where institutional racism is rife. As was confirmed by the landmark

Macpherson report that was published in February 1999 following the unprovoked racist attack by a gang of young white men who brutally murdered eighteen-year-old Stephen Lawrence whilst he was crossing the street on the evening of 22 April 1993. In this case two people were charged but by the end of July 1993 all charges were dropped (not until 3 January 2012 were two of the perpetrators convicted of murder). The report concluded that the investigation 'was marred by a combination of professional incompetence, institutional racism and a failure of leadership by senior officers'. The report defined institutional racism as,

> The collective failure of an organisation to provide an appropriate and professional service to people because of their colour, culture, or ethnic origin. It can be seen or detected in processes, attitudes and behaviour which amount to discrimination through unwitting prejudice, ignorance, thoughtlessness and racist stereotyping that disadvantage minority ethnic people.[6]

Black victims and survivors face racism, bias and a lack of cultural awareness in our criminal justice system. Their experiences are often invalidated due to 'lack of evidence' as bruising isn't as visible as it is on white women; they are victim-blamed and not believed due to the racial stereotype of Black women being in some way stronger than white women. The reporting of Black men will often lead to a backlash for the victim from Black communities, families or religious figures, which in turn keeps survivors in abusive homes and pushes them to silence and further into isolation. The impact of the Windrush scandal, combined with hostile immigration policies, further isolates African and Caribbean heritage survivors, pushing them away from seeking institutional support if they are in fear of deportation or losing their immigration status.

Many of the experiences that I have documented and shared in this chapter can be understood within the framework of 'intersectionality'. The term intersectionality has become a buzzword in recent years, with its increasingly popular and mainstream usage. It is employed by modern feminists to highlight the crossover of distinct discriminations, which might include sexism, racism, ableism or classism. The term itself was coined in a legal academic paper by Kimberlé Crenshaw in 1989, who defines it as 'a lens through which you can see where power comes and collides, where it interlocks and intersects'. Writer Reni Eddo-Lodge, who met Crenshaw when she was visiting London, recorded Crenshaw's comments in her book *Why I'm No Longer Talking to White People About Race*. Crenshaw shared that the work began upon her realisation that African American women were not recognised as having experienced discrimination on the basis of both their race and their gender. She argued that the experiences of Black women were being marginalised and ignored as the courts claimed that if you don't experience racism as a Black man does or sexism as a white women does then you have not been discriminated against. She described it as a problem of 'sameness and difference' as Black women's unique experiences of discrimination were not accommodated or acknowledged by the law. This understanding led her to intersectionality, exploring the ways in which different forms of discrimination intersect to create obstacles to equality.[7]

This way of thinking has long been explored by Black writers, activists and feminists before there was a term to define these experiences. bell hooks, for example, argued in *Ain't I a Woman: Black women and feminism* that the process begins with a woman's acceptance that they have been socialised to be racist, classist and sexist, in varying degrees, and that we cannot merely label ourselves feminists but must consciously choose to work to eradicate within ourselves a 'legacy of negative socialization'.[8] She claims that many women, especially white women who have been at the forefront of the movement, have appropriated feminism to serve their own ends. Instead of resigning herself to this appropriation she instead chooses 'to re-appropriate the term "feminism" to focus on the fact that to be "feminist" in any authentic sense of the term is to want for all people, female and male, liberation from sexist role patterns, domination, and oppression'.[9] hooks champions a universal and inclusive feminism that is uplifting to all – all genders, all backgrounds and all skin colours. In order to work meaningfully towards this goal, it is crucial that in our thinking and our activism we pay attention to, and highlight, difference as opposed to sameness, in addressing experiences of discrimination. The first and second wave feminist movements and the #MeToo movement have been criticised for a discourse of common oppression and an overemphasis on unity; a presupposition that all women share the same universal experiences of discrimination.[10] In *The Right to Sex*, Amia Srinivasan cautions her readers in their understanding and application of intersectionality. For Srinivasan, if intersectionality is reduced to merely a 'due consideration of the various axes of oppression and privilege: race, class, sexuality, disability and so on', then we will 'forego its power as a theoretical practical orientation'. She writes that if we do this, 'what all members of the relevant group have in common is a movement that will best serve those members of the group who are least oppressed'.[11]

This played out during #MeToo as the interests and experiences of the Black and minority ethnic communities, represented by the movement's African American founder Tarana Burke, were eclipsed by the stories of white Hollywood actresses that dominated the media focus. Tarana Burke herself has been vocal in criticising the movement's evolution and how the concern and outrage elicited by the famous revelations of white Hollywood actresses were not consistent across racial lines. This pattern of prioritising the voices of the privileged can also be seen in the evolution of Everyone's Invited in the media. When Everyone's Invited initially hit the headlines in March 2021, because of my background of having attended a private boarding school, there was a huge focus on elite schools in and around London. In the first few weeks, the testimonies and voices of survivors who attended private schools were most focused on in the media. Whilst at the time we did our best to widen the conversation by insisting in every interview that this is a universal problem that exists in all of society and therefore in all schools – state funded or private – there was still a huge emphasis on a small number of schools that educate England's most privileged, wealthy and elite. Later, as the movement grew, the focus did widen and the media began to acknowledge and platform the stories from survivors of all backgrounds, including some of the most marginalised in society.

We must endeavour to understand and acknowledge difference. Too much emphasis on sameness enables the eclipsing of the most marginalised voices, which are too often superseded by the white and privileged who have, in the past, situated their interests as the primary focus. As a woman who is half white and who is socio-economically privileged, it is imperative in my work and in my activism that I am conscious of this privilege and, most importantly, do everything in my power to listen to, elevate and then follow the voices that are too often forgotten; the voices of the most marginalised survivors of sexual violence. Only then can we hope to achieve true equality, in advocating for a movement that is universal, inclusive, uplifting and inviting to all.

Movements Making Movements

Everyone's Invited began in June 2020, a few months into the first UK Covid-19 pandemic lockdown, in my dad's flat. At the time, I was interested in the power of testimony. The roar of the Black Lives Matter movement was still fresh in the public conscience. I remember reading countless personal stories and accounts of racism online. It was a defining moment of exposure that pushed the world first to introspection and then action. Social media is an abundant and powerful tool, allowing the sharing of information that galvanised a global movement. Instagram and Twitter quickly became hosts for a spectrum of experiences that ranged from everyday racism, microaggressions and systemic racism in society's institutions, to the police brutality and violence systematically perpetrated against Black bodies. This oppression and its insidious quality was exposed in a tidal wave that swept across mainstream media, the internet and social media apps. Violence and suffering were forced into public view. I began to see the many parallels between racism and sexism. These systems of oppression are woven into the fabric of modern society, embedded deep into the public subconscious, manifesting at every level of society in the form of unconscious bias and impulses; from our daily interactions to the structures of government and institutions, to representation on the screen, to the inner workings of the police and criminal justice systems. Dehumanisation, discrimination and prejudice are the common denominators that unite racism and sexism as systems of oppression. And yet, at this time of the Black Lives Matter movement, I couldn't help but wonder why this outrage elicited by racial injustice did not extend to that of gender or why the dehumanisation of Black bodies was rightly met with furious anger and collective action yet the dehumanisation of an entire gender was and still is permissible, socially acceptable and normalised?

Whilst I was living with my American grandparents in France during the second UK Covid-19 lockdown, I had many conversations about feminism and racism with my grandmother who is the trailblazing matriarch on my dad's side (my white side) of the family. As a young woman, she was heavily engaged in activism during the second wave of feminism and the civil rights movement in the US. Speaking to her at length about my work with Everyone's Invited, she observed how the patterns of history were re-emerging as the discourse of women's rights increased in the aftermath of Black Lives Matter, just as the civil rights movement had acted as a precursor to second wave feminism in the 1960s. She brought to my attention the infamous moment in 1964 where civil rights organiser Stokely Carmichael, a prominent member of the movement's Student Nonviolent Coordinating Committee, was asked what the position of women was in the SNCC, to which he responded, 'prone'. Emerging in response to the entrenched sexism and misogyny of the 1960s activist movements were the feminist critiques of the New Left. This would later become the Women's liberation movement of the 1970s. Throughout history, campaigns for women's rights are often born out of the campaigns for racial justice. In July 1848 at Seneca Falls, New York, abolitionists Elizabeth Cady Stanton and Lucretia Mott organised an assembly for the first great women's convention that launched the women's suffrage movement in the US out of the anger they felt after facing rejection and discrimination when attempting to join the fight against slavery. When they tried to attend the world's anti-slavery convention in London, they were met with discrimination by the male-dominated organisation who refused to seat female delegates. One historian wrote that Stanton and Mott 'began to see similarities between their own circumscribed status and that of slaves'.[1] Moreover, both Josephine Butler and English suffrage leader Emmeline Pankhurst came from abolitionist families. Some of the most influential writers and feminists from the 1980s until the present day are Black women whose work interrogates the harms caused by a white-dominated feminist discourse, and explores the intersections and combinations of oppression of race, class and gender – intersectionality before the term was coined. Just a few of these writers include Angela Davis, bell hooks, Michele Wallace, Audre Lorde, Toni Morrison, Roxane Gay and Chimamanda Ngozi Adichie.

There is a centuries-old pattern of oppression that has endured through time, history and across continents. A group who is the object of oppression at times can also choose to oppress another group to claim back their power. They find security in their dominance and oppression of others. Racism is a system of oppression in which we are all complicit. Born and raised in a white, patriarchal society, we have been socialised, whether we like it or not, to harbour racist impulses. Sexism is also a system of oppression in which we are all complicit. Born and raised in a white, patriarchal society, we have been socialised, whether we like it or not, to harbour sexist impulses. Writing in the *New Yorker*, critic Katy Waldman discusses sociologist Robin DiAngelo's examination of 'white fragility' that prevents white Americans from confronting racism.

> In DiAngelo's almost epidemiological vision of white racism, our minds and bodies play host to a pathogen that seeks to replicate itself, sickening us in the process. Like a mutating virus, racism shape-shifts in order to stay alive; when its explicit expression becomes taboo, it hides in coded language. Nor does prejudice disappear when people decide that they will

no longer tolerate it. It just looks for ways to avoid detection.[2]

Much like racism, sexism and misogyny move around and through us in the same way. Deeply entrenched in society, it's in the air we breathe. It 'shape-shifts' and 'mutates' to avoid detection, lingering in the language we use, in our relationships and within the institutions we navigate. A 'pathogen' that spreads, it is passed on from generation to generation and exacerbated by the changing world around us, mutating into new, more extreme forms with the rise of social media and online pornography.

DiAngelo claims,

> The most effective adaptation of racism over time is the idea that racism is a conscious bias held by mean people. This good/bad binary, positing a world of evil racists and compassionate non-racists, is itself a racist construct, enabling systemic injustice and imbuing racism with such shattering moral meaning that white people, especially progressives, cannot bear to confront their collusion.[3]

The 'good/bad' binary perspective of life, the viewing of individuals as one-dimensional, inflexible beings, completely ignores the complex existence of humanity. We are constantly being formed and re-formed by our experiences, trauma and social interactions. We are capable of both good and bad, right and wrong. We make mistakes and we learn. Reducing rapists to evil monsters and the rest to innocent bystanders works only to alleviate our own moral culpability and social responsibility. We, who have looked the other way in the face of abuse, excused a friend or family member of their predatory behaviour because they're 'such a great guy'; we, whose first instinct is to doubt and question a survivor when they come forward to share their story. The inability to face reality, to look the brutal face of racial violence in the eye, can also be seen in the refusal of many to confront and engage with survivors and their stories of sexual violence. The plugging of the ears, the defensive shutting down of the dialogue, these are all ways of brushing the unsavoury, ugly stories under the carpet and out of sight. As human beings, we feel safer when there is distance between us and suffering. When pain is boxed up, locked and taken far away, we can carry on in our blissful ignorance and pretend as though it doesn't exist.

On 25 May 2020 the white police officer who knelt on the neck of a Black man named George Floyd incited a global reckoning on racism, white privilege and violence perpetrated against Black people. The world was finally beginning to understand how the racist beliefs that we, as a society, have been conditioned into adopting lead to racist impulses and prejudices, which in turn bleed into bigoted behaviours, corrupt structures, racist laws, police brutality and, ultimately, murder. This understanding of the connection between racism and racial violence informed my understanding of the connection between sexism and sexual violence. Everything is interconnected.

There is a male police officer nicknamed 'the rapist' by his colleagues. He is known for making women feel 'uncomfortable'. He is part of a WhatsApp group with five other male police officers where they have shared racist and misogynistic content. He is arrested for flashing his genitals in public back in 2015 but, despite this incident, he is hired by the police in 2018. The checks carried out by the police force were reportedly 'not done correctly'. In 2021, he is caught for the second time, indecently exposing himself in his car at a McDonald's drive-thru. Weeks later, on 3 March 2021, he falsely employed Covid-19 protocol, his ID and handcuffs to abduct a young woman in her thirties. He raped and murdered her. Women's fear of violence intensified across the country; they feared for their safety on the streets. The politicians suggested an early curfew for women and more 'plain clothed' officers to patrol the streets, nightclubs and bars. The police advised them to 'shout or wave a bus down' or 'call the police' if they 'don't trust the police'. The women congregated at a vigil to mourn her death on Clapham Common. The mourners are handcuffed and pushed forcibly to the ground by male police officers. Their knees crushing their bodies down. Face down.

Backlash

In 2021, I was invited to speak on a panel that endeavoured to both highlight female achievement and address the concerns and desires of working women. I could feel my nerves scissoring as we waited to be called on stage. Although I'd spoken publicly on many occasions since the explosion of Everyone's Invited, I was still nervous every time I had to speak in front of a crowd. I was moved by the journeys of the other women, their own insights and advice on cultivating the resilience needed to achieve their goals. I spoke a little bit about my journey and shared how Everyone's Invited didn't really begin as a big dream of mine. It started with me sharing my story about something that had happened to me. And once I shared this story there was an outpouring of stories, and when I saw how many people had been through the same thing, had suffered in the same way, I wanted to do everything I could to expose the problem and eradicate it. The dream came as a consequence of this act of sharing.

After we finished there was a break for lunch. We were all in good spirits, many people had approached us to talk about Everyone's Invited. I was moved by their kindness and still a little shaky from all the adrenaline from speaking on the panel. As I was eating my lunch, a white woman in her late forties asked if I had a spare moment to speak with her. She had a blank face and stern demeanour, and began to question me about Everyone's Invited. 'What do you think about the impact of Everyone's Invited?' she asked. I went on to talk about the thousands of survivors we had empowered and helped across the country to come forward; how the NSPCC helpline that was created in response to the testimonies had taken hundreds of calls since we launched the platform. I spoke of the Ofsted review, our work with government ministers, the Department for Education and the Home Office. Yet her face remained firm, cold and blank. My words didn't seem to reach her.

'What about the boys?' she asked. 'Don't you think you've ruined some of their lives and reputations? Do you know that my son is scared to do anything now; he doesn't even know how to speak to a girl because of you.'

I was thrown. Dealing with backlash is of course a huge part of my job, trying to reach people who don't agree or understand the perspective of survivors is a crucially important part of the work of Everyone's Invited. However, I was caught off-guard by this woman who had gone out of her way to accost me, at a women's summit, created for women to support and empower women.

'You are making life hard for the boys. Think about how this is impacting them,' she continued. I explained that our work is for everyone, that we are supporting all survivors of all backgrounds and genders. The work is about spotlighting the experiences of victims and survivors – of which the vast majority happen to be women and girls. We have always led with empathy; empathy for all, including boys and men who are victims of this culture too. But that wasn't enough for her.

'How do you know the testimonies are real? How can you check?' I said that it was exactly this kind of thinking – the assumption that survivors are lying – that we are trying to change. This way of thinking is responsible for silencing victims of rape and abuse. But she wasn't listening. She wasn't engaging with what I was saying.

'What about my son's reputation? This accusation will stay with him for the rest of his life.'

'And what about the girls?' I asked. 'What about their lives?' At this point the woman was seething with rage. It completely knocked me off balance because I could not have anticipated that level of hostility at this kind of event. On my way out, another woman approached me. 'Thank you so much for your work. I'm a lawyer who works in employment and education and I've been following the campaign. I just wanted to tell you how important your work is.' I opened my mouth to respond but found myself overwhelmed and unable to speak, bursting into tears in a room full of people. I stood there like a sore thumb, with an ugly red crying face in my big bright blue dress and pink shoes.

• • •

This was nothing new. Mothers of boys were the most vocal group who led the charge to discredit the validity of the testimonies. Back in March 2021, when Everyone's Invited first began to explode in the press, my colleague Wendy was met with fierce doubt, anger, and disbelief. Wendy Mair has been an instrumental force in the journey of Everyone's Invited, and has supported the movement in all areas. With fierce passion and purpose she has driven the direction of the movement by my side. Since the early days, we have worked closely together, dealing with the over-whelming explosion of national and international media and press requests that we received over the course of the initial months. Mothers rang her up to question her intentions. They pressed her daily: 'Are you sure you're doing the right thing?' They accused her of 'going too far'. They dismissed the work as 'reckless' and argued that the testimonies were 'fake' or 'false', and claimed because they were 'anonymous' this threw their validity into question. They were ferocious in their arguments, insisting that the abuse in the testimonies was 'exaggerated' and did not merit the attention that it was receiving in the press. Others focused their concern around the 'sexualised content' of the testimonies on the website. 'The testimonies are not age appropriate; anyone can have access to these stories.' More malicious arguments were strategically employed in an attempt to silence us, to stop the publication of the testimonies. 'What if an innocent boy who is falsely accused commits suicide because of you, you will be personally responsible.' One mother said there 'will be blood' on our hands. When things first began to go viral, the team and I received a series of letters that disturbed us. The letters were submitted anonymously to the website and constituted a series of threats personally addressed to myself and the volunteers. In them, the same individual demanded that we create another counter on the website, not for the testimonies, but for the number of suicides of boys accused that we would be 'personally responsible for'.

It is interesting to note that the backlash I received from my peers was much smaller than the backlash we received from parents. Young people seemed more open to the testimonies, most boys and young men being receptive to experiences of their female peers that differed from their own. They also lived it, they went through it, coming of age in a modern sexual landscape that was defined by the mainstreaming of hardcore pornography and the age of social media. However, it is important to note that backlash from younger boys did exist, notably from those who took issue with a campaign which challenged their behaviour and status quo. In June 2022, journalist Damian Whitworth wrote a feature piece in the *Times* that investigated the impact of Everyone's Invited 'a year on'. In it, he interviews a girl who had been shown WhatsApp messages between groups of boys from a west London school who 'wanted to rape the person who started the site' as 'they were angry that their behaviour was being questioned'.[1] Some parents from the older generations were more rigidly committed to their views and understanding of the world, viewing their own experiences alone as objective reality. Throughout the course of the campaign it has proved more difficult to shift the perspectives of parents than it has for young adults, university students, and teenagers at school. The most fierce backlash has come from individuals who are staunchly fixed in their beliefs. People who are unwilling to try to understand, or to empathise with a different perspective from their own. Influencing their perspective and world view are age-old rape myths that are deeply ingrained in society, even more rigidly in the older generations who have held these beliefs for decades.

Writing in the *Spectator*, journalist Melanie McDonagh called it a 'wretched site' and dismissed the testimonies as 'sordid'. She highlights how the anonymous nature of the platform leads to 'no opportunity for the alleged perpetrators to put their side: just a safe online space for girls to sound off, on their own terms'.[2] McDonagh is misleading in her implication that the scales are unfairly weighted towards the victim's perspective. What she completely misses is the reality that victims, in a society that stigmatises sexual violence to such an extreme extent, have never before had the opportunity to openly share their perspective. Her focus and priority remain on that of the accused. Moreover, there are no named 'alleged perpetrators' in the testimonies, Everyone's Invited is and has always been completely anonymous. What she and many others fail to understand is that the anonymity is crucial in allowing survivors to share openly in a world where sexual violence is still shrouded in stigma, shame and humiliation. Anonymity allows survivors to speak openly, and freely, and in many cases for the very first time. The essential function of the website has always been to provide a safe place for those who have suffered from abuse to share their stories. These are not allegations or formal reports. Some critics, namely the 'not all men' camp, claimed that by platforming the stories of survivors we were slandering all men and boys, generalising them all as sexual predators. When an individual responds in this way they redirect a discussion about misogyny, sexism and rape culture to instead be about how none of it is their responsibility. Journalist Jess Zimmerman wrote on this in *Time* magazine. 'The Not-All-Man hero and his minions are paralyzingly obsessed with protecting their own self-concept, to a degree that prevents them from engaging in sincere discussion.'[3] 'Not all men' as an argument works to shut down the dialogue, to eradicate the problem from view, and to absolve all blame and responsibility. Yes, not all men are guilty of assault or rape but all men and women are unavoidably sexist because we have been socialised in a sexist environment, all men and women are complicit in violence when we live in a culture that excuses predatory and abusive behaviour and fails to hold abusers and rapists accountable.

It is an age-old sexist societal trope to prioritise, value and protect the white male perspective at all costs. For many, the protection of boys, their reputation and 'bright futures' remain the priority. Arguing that girls get drunk at parties, behave like 'sluts', and regret it the next day, accusing the victims of lying and making up false allegations. 'You have destroyed their lives and reputations' was the instinctive response of many mothers. Protecting the reputation of their sons took precedence over the lives, futures, rights and safety of all victims. Some mothers blamed us for the treatment of their sons who were being called out for their bad behaviour, complaining that their boys were being bullied and ostracised in response to accusations that were being made against them. Journalist Katie Strick wrote a piece in the *Evening Standard* entitled '"Being a boy is one of the hardest things to be in London now" – the devastating Everyone's Invited backlash begins'. In it, she interviews distraught mother *Rebecca, who claims that her son is 'now terrified of going near another girl again'.

Emerald Fennell's BAFTA-winning film *Promising Young Woman* (2020) is a fearless rallying cry for a new perspective on sexual assault. One piece of dialogue sums up the double standards at play.

'It's every guy's worst nightmare getting accused like that.'

'Can you guess what every woman's worst nightmare is?'

Just like the film's inverting title, *Promising Young Woman* (an allusion to the infamous Brock Turner case wherein which Turner, an accused rapist, was referred to by the judge as a 'promising young man') is packed with tropes, scenes and moments of dialogue that flip the script, forcing its audience to view things from the victim's perspective. Writing a review of the film in *Harper's Bazaar*, Marie-Claire Chappet notes how this flipping of perspective 'directly addresses the cruel double standards of these situations . . . how a woman's reputation is enough to damn her, but a man's reputation must be protected at all costs. It asks us what weight we give to the female promise over male.'[4] Time and time again we have seen this, a relentless prioritising of the perpetrator's life over the victim's.

This priority is most evident within the criminal justice system which is underpinned by the fundamental legal principle of the presumption of innocence of anyone accused of a crime. Even before a rape trial begins, the odds are overwhelmingly stacked in favour of the accused who is presumed innocent, with the burden of proof resting on the victim. The victim's harrowing ordeal in the aftermath of assault is fiercely interrogated in Suzie Miller's one-woman play, *Prima Facie*. I was invited to attend a performance and speak on a panel on stage alongside barristers and legal experts during its run at the Harold Pinter Theatre starring actor Jodie Comer. I was astonished, mesmerised and outraged by Jodie Comer's performance. *Prima Facie* tells the story of a young defence barrister who is raped by a colleague and is suddenly confronted with the crushing reality that a legal system that she has dedicated her life to upholding and defending cannot deliver justice for a survivor of rape. The play is arresting in its confrontation of an entrenched patriarchal legal system of truth – created, defined and upheld by men. In 2016, twenty-year-old Stanford swimmer Brock Turner was convicted, sentenced by Santa Clara County Superior Court Judge Aaron Persky to six months in county jail[5] (he served only three) on three felony charges of sexual assault of Chanel Miller in 2015.[6] This priority of the accused's perspective can be read in a statement that his father, Dan Turner, penned to the judge. He wrote:

> He will never be his happy go lucky self with that easy going personality and welcoming smile . . . You can see this in his face, the way he walks, his weakened voice, his lack of appetite . . . His life will never be the one that he dreamed about and worked so hard to achieve. That is a steep price to pay for 20 minutes of action out of his 20 plus years of life.

Such an astonishing letter elicited immediate outrage across social media, with many users on Twitter alleging rape culture as displayed by Turner's likening of the sexual assault to '20 minutes of action'. Miller's experience in this letter is absent, a stark contrast to Miller's own victim impact statement, which makes a point of acknowledging the detrimental impact

176

of the assault on both the victim and the perpetrator's lives. 'You and me,' she writes, 'you are the cause, I am the effect, you have dragged me through this hell with you . . . nobody wins.' Sexual trauma is life-changing and can completely transform the victim's life path, destroying their mental health and relationships, crippling their future prospects, and capacity to live their life. The lasting and life-changing impact of the victim is harrowingly conveyed in Miller's 7,137-word viral victim impact statement.

> Your damage was concrete; stripped of titles, degrees, enrollment. My damage was internal, unseen, I carry it with me. You took away my worth, my privacy, my energy, my time, my safety, my intimacy, my confidence, my own voice, until today.[7]

Miller's words are powerful, extinguishing the notion that there are 'winners' and 'losers' in the victim's traumatic aftermath of sexual violence. Seizing control over her own narrative, finding the power in her voice, and flipping the script to the victim's perspective are the driving forces of her full impact statement. The suffering victim's face is often, as Miller states, 'internal', obscured from view, but nevertheless they too often endure insurmountable suffering in the wake of an event that can be fundamentally life-changing for them. The profound impact on the victim's life as conveyed in Miller's impact statement makes Dan Turner's use of the sexual pun '20 minutes of action' even more disturbing. In minimising the act of sexual assault, he normalises such violence. Should my son be punished for this? he asks. Is my son not above the law and moral order? he implies. Certain kinds of boys and men do in fact exist above the law, as is so often demonstrated by those who are positioned at the apex of power. By the Brett Kavanaughs and the Donald Trumps, who after *that* infamous recording still managed to ascend to the most powerful office in the free world. 'I just start kissing them. It's like a magnet. Just kiss. I don't even wait. And when you're a star, they let you do it. You can do anything . . . Grab 'em by the pussy.'[8] Marie-Claire Chappet states that we must ask ourselves who exists above the law and who sits beneath it? Whose bright futures do we protect? Whose lives are considered sacrosanct and whose are rendered disposable? Whose promise do we preserve and who is 'exaggerating', 'overreacting' and 'ruining the fun'? *Promising Young Woman* is about centring the victim's perspective. Everyone's Invited is doing the same. We are trying to 'flip the script'. We are exposing the other side of the story. By platforming the experiences of victims, we are endeavouring to shift a societal perspective and narrative that has, since the beginning of time, privileged the lives of the accused over the lives of victims and survivors.

Of course, this backlash is a fraction of the picture: overwhelmingly we had a moving positive response, and were astonished by the level of support we received, the allies gained, the community we built, and the collective action and activism we inspired at an individual and collective level from all corners of British society. For the most part, the work of Everyone's Invited was overwhelmingly supported by the majority of the girls I grew up with. Whilst powerful, the level of support garnered is also indicative of the severity of the problem; how is it possible that every girl I grew up with could relate in some way or another to these stories of pain and trauma? Why did these stories hit home so powerfully? Why does every girl and woman have some experience of trauma of some form within the spectrum of sexual violence? These are questions I raise to encourage you, the reader, to confront a distressing reality, to be willing to put yourself in the shoes of the survivor, to be willing to listen. The backlash we've received comes from those who lack the volition to engage in the empathy needed to understand, those who are fixated on their reality, their understanding of the world and the maintenance of the status quo.

Almost every girl I've ever known, in my immediate and wider social circles, mutual friends, friends of friends, all stood up to support Everyone's Invited. My posts and account went viral multiple times as countless individuals reposted screenshots of the Instagram page and website imploring their followers, friends, parents and communities to read the testimonies on Everyone's Invited. It was empowering and moving to see so many people support survivors with incredible passion, and be committed to raising awareness and reducing the suffering that so many had experienced. Rape culture, sexual violence and harassment were fervently discussed at dinner tables, in coffee shops, at the library and in pubs across the country. Countless friends and friends of friends messaged me or approached me in person to tell me all about the discussions, arguments and debates they were having amongst themselves. The girls were loud and unapologetic in their support. Speaking from personal trauma and experiences, many felt empowered to openly share personal stories online, writing and performing poetry about their experiences of harassment and assault they faced whilst at school and university. I was moved and still am blown away by this level of bravery in their ability to transform the vulnerability of pain and suffering into hopeful and moving works of art.

Personally, I have found this process to be a crucial form of therapy, a way to make sense of my own trauma and come to terms with my experiences. Writing, rewriting and sharing these small creations with my loved ones has helped me move forward on my healing journey. In her personal manifesto *Misfits* (2021), Michaela Coel writes about the process of creating the TV series *I May Destroy You* (2020), a groundbreaking exploration of the impact of sexual trauma in the aftermath of sexual violence. 'Like any other experience I've found traumatic, it's been therapeutic to write about it, and actively twist a narrative of pain into one of hope, and even humour. And to be able to share it with you, as part of a fictional drama on television, because I think transparency helps.'[9]

Transparency does help. It helps to know that your experience isn't one in a million, that it's not rare, that many others have shared the trauma that you may have felt. It was moving to witness the blossoming of an empowered community of survivors and allies who supported the cause without shame, with so much love and empathy for those who have suffered. The level of support and sense of community that emerged as Everyone's Invited grew was both intimate and affirming.

In the first few weeks of March 2021 current and former pupils from secondary schools took action, banding together in solidarity to collect dossiers from individual schools which they sent in open letters to heads and governors. Very disturbingly, an overwhelming theme that dominates these dossiers is an institutional priority to protect the school's reputation over the well-being and safety of their own pupils. Time and time again we have seen this in responses to and the treatment of victims who have suffered from abuse and violence in both schools and universities. Priorities are devastatingly misaligned when image, profit, and reputation take precedence over human rights and child safety. It is heartbreaking to truly understand and come to terms with the astronomical failures of these institutions to protect and safeguard their pupils.

The dossiers compiled by pupils documented a spectrum of experiences ranging from low level harassment to coercion, rape and online sexual abuse. The dossiers described the deeply entrenched cultures of misogyny and sexual abuse in institutions, exposing the devastating failures of staff to adequately deal with allegations. In many cases, members of staff were accused of re-traumatising pupils by failing to hold abusers accountable in the absence of appropriate punishments. Some teachers and senior staff members were accused of victim-blaming pupils and forcing them to sit in the same classrooms with their rapists. In one school a pupil recounted how the boys banded together to support another boy who had been accused of rape, chanting his name in support at house parties and on school premises whilst shaming and ostracising his victim. In the aftermath of rape and assault some former pupils recount receiving death threats from their perpetrators' friends and being bullied and isolated by their peers. Another case alleged that a male pupil had stolen the identity of a female pupil and posed as a lesbian on a dating app where he solicited intimate photos from underage girls. Threats and rape jokes were embedded in everyday school life. 'The boy actually joked about raping me publicly and no one cared,' says one entry. 'I was sexually assaulted and groped on a school trip,' reads another. Another recounts how a male pupil projected imagery of a female pupil on the school whiteboard in front of a staff member, asking the class whether they'd 'smash or not'. Many mixed sixth forms were accused of subjecting new female pupils to a tunnel of harassment as they rated girls entering the school on their first day. One girl wrote about a harrowing and humiliating experience at a house party where a group of boys from an all-boys school held her down and stripped her of her bra and T-shirt. This daily reality was described as 'ritualised sexual harassment and assault culture', which took place in all the environments young people navigated, at house parties, on the street, in school corridors and in school toilets. One former female pupil called an all-boys school in London 'A hotbed of sexual violence'. Another male pupil wrote to his former head, deeming the school a 'breeding ground for sexual predators'. He highlighted how isolated incidents were exacerbated by peers who sustained a toxic culture of misogyny.

In almost every story, experiences of assault, revenge pornography and slut shaming were exacerbated by the aggressors' friends, young men who laughed at stories of sexual violence, who shared illicit photos of teenage girls without consent, who stood by as their mates ruined lives. These accounts are as heartbreaking as they are outraging.

It is crucial to understand how inaction directly enables abuse. If you stand by in silence, and do nothing in the face of abuse, you too are indirectly responsible for the victim's plight. Moreover, the treatment of the victim by her peers and community after an incident can in many cases have an even more severe impact than the original incident. Re-traumatisation is a common experience that many survivors are forced to endure as they are too often disbelieved, discarded, shamed, ridiculed and humiliated by their school communities, teachers and peers alike.

School should be a safe place where young people are free to grow, learn and develop without the fear of violence and harassment each day. It is heartbreaking to come to an understanding that schools and universities are not safe places for young people. These are formative years, young people deserve to make the most of their time at school, their safety should be guaranteed, a priority and an absolute. What we have exposed at Everyone's Invited is how far away we are from this reality. We cannot let this continue, it is both unbelievable and unacceptable that this is happening in the UK in 2022.

Encouraged and outraged by the severity and scale of the problem and the increasing public awareness stimulated by the explosion of media attention, protests and school walkouts were organised and staged by pupils across London. The girls raised placards that read:

We stand strong, we stand tall and most importantly we stand together.

Sexual violence is not bullying. It is a violation of human rights.

Girls should feel safe at school.

On 22 March 2021, I received a moving email sharing an open letter written to a headteacher and school governors. Signed by 450 former male pupils, the letter was an honest, thoughtful testimony of remorse that called for immediate and 'concrete' action from the school and its governors to conduct a thorough review on institutional rape culture and explore solutions to eradicate it.

> It would be disingenuous for any of us to claim that we are surprised by such personal testimonies. Too many of us have stood by and failed to respond to stories which circulate in the dark about instances of sexual assault. And all of us, to varying degrees, have contributed to the 'Misogyny, slut shaming, victim blaming, and [even] sexual harassment' that enable – and are symptomatic of – pervasive rape culture. We all must do better . . . We must all take this opportunity to reflect deeply on how we, as individuals and as a school community, enable power structures which implicitly entitle some to take advantage of their peers, and how we contribute to a society which chooses to trivialise sexual violence. As signatories, we recognise our own roles in normalising rape culture at the school.

I have included this extract, contrary to what many might believe or assume, to show you that this is not and has never been a 'gender war'. Fathers, teenage boys, and countless men have been moved by reading the testimonies and are some of the biggest advocates for change and supporters of our work. As Everyone's Invited continued to grow I began to receive countless Instagram direct messages, Facebook messages, and emails from boys I grew up with in London. Many of the messages expressed an urgent desire to help, many expressed remorse and regret, many thanked me and expressed their gratitude in opening their eyes to the reality of these experiences. They admitted that they didn't understand at the time, they were desensitised and unaware of the gravity of their actions or inaction. They spoke of a peer on peer 'normalisation' of predatory behaviour, how the sexism and misogyny were so deeply embedded and ingrained in the way they were raised, and in the environments they grew up in, that the behaviour was a subconscious 'reflex'. They said the act of reading the testimonies had transformed their perspective around these issues, forcing introspection, and leading to an understanding of how, as a bystander, as a friend who bears witness to bad behaviour and does nothing, they are complicit in sustaining an environment that is conducive to sexual violence. Many wrote about socialisation and how it was a part of the culture, part of the way young people interacted with one another. The boys I spoke to told me that misogynistic subcultures were a form of bonding for them. It was how they communicated, entertained one another, and collected clout. One boy shared that he believed these behaviours were 'endemic' amongst the boys he grew up with. 'I don't think the people that are unfollowing you and reacting badly are doing it because they disagree with you, I think they're doing it because they recognise exactly what you're talking about but can't face up to the fact that they were/are still complicit,' he said.

In May 2021, I was invited to speak about Everyone's Invited at the Oxford Union, a debating society with a long tradition of hosting prominent public figures. Having never spoken in public before, I was nervous, but had no intention of passing up such an opportunity. Most of the backlash we had received around this time was centred around our use of the words 'rape culture' so I was keen to address and explore this in my speech.

Rape culture is a spectrum of attitudes, beliefs and behaviours in a society that have the effect of making rape permissible. Behaviours such as whistling at passing women, girls being reduced to ratings on a list, being groped at an office party; these are behaviours that have the cumulative effect of dehumanising individuals, and when any individual is dehumanised they become vulnerable to sexual violence. Gateway behaviours, when left unchecked by passive bystanders and wider communities, can lead to criminal acts such as rape and sexual assault. This is an environment where norms and institutions protect rapists, where victims are blamed, shamed, and ostracised by their communities and peers for their own assaults. Rape culture exists when survivors are not believed by their families, communities, peers, and police officers when they come forward. Sexual violence continues to happen because society, the laws, police, institutions and criminal justice system fail to hold rapists and abusers accountable for their behaviour. Official figures reported in *The Times* and the *Guardian* state that of the 61,158 rape reports in the year 2020 to June recorded by police forces in England and Wales, only 1.4 per cent – equivalent to one in seventy rape cases – led to a suspect being charged or summonsed.[10] This is the reality we are living in, a reality where rape claims have soared and charges have hit a record low. Where the crime of rape itself has effectively been decriminalised as victims can expect a one in seventy chance of their rapist being convicted. Rape is the product or consequence of a rape culture.

I gave my speech and another backlash in the comment section of the YouTube video of it duly followed. Despite our efforts to explain the term 'rape culture', many people were fixated on the word 'rape', shutting their ears to anything else I had to say, let alone engaging in the dialogue.

Anyone who believes there is a 'rape culture' (where language is bent so far as to include things like whistling at passing women – not ok, but not rape) is utterly, utterly delusional. One of the things we learnt about this so-called 'rape culture' is that it includes things like teenage boys making lists of which girls they find most attractive. Really?

This is a typical example of the feedback I received.

Change in any form, in any society, has throughout history instigated resistance and backlash. We experienced it in the aftermath of Black Lives Matter, in the counter rallying cry that 'All Lives Matter'. White fragility emerged, naked, bold and aggressive from a place of insecurity, an inability to come to terms with its own complacency in the systemic and institutional oppression of Black people. The devil's advocates and conservatives launched their attacks, eager to defend a status quo that positioned them at the apex of society's social order. Why would they want change when they stand to benefit most from the status quo? Fixated on protesting their innocence, they failed to engage in the dialogue, to listen to Black and minority groups, to find within themselves the empathy needed that would allow them to understand how we, raised in a society where whiteness is the norm, are all responsible and complicit in racism.

When #MeToo exploded in 2017, it didn't take long for the backlash and criticism to mount. In response to the French #MeToo, *#BalanceTonPorc*, a group of high-profile, white, elitist French women, including actress Catherine Deneuve and writer Catherine Millet, launched an infamous counter-attack, publishing a notorious letter in *Le Monde* that claimed the movement had gone too far declaring it 'a hatred of men and sexuality'.[11] They wrote that arguments protecting women were being used to 'lock them in their roles as eternal victims, poor little things at the mercy of phallocentric demons'. They brazenly defended 'a freedom to *bother*, indispensable to sexual freedom',[12] using the word *importuner*, which ranges in meaning from bothering someone to seriously disturbing them. The group implied that sexual aggression was an integral part of the dating process and to deny men this freedom is to threaten the game of seduction. They implied that sexual harassment is an inevitability in the pursuit of love and romance.

We are living in the age of polarisation; a divide that has increasingly revealed itself in the cultural wars elicited in the wake of Brexit, Donald Trump's presidency, and the Black Lives Matter and #MeToo movements. In the unforgiving landscape of cancel culture, underlined by incendiary anger and hostility, our world has become increasingly divided and the bridges between opposing viewpoints are broken. Dismissive responses to 'rape culture' and the survivor testimonies display a lack of volition to listen and an unwillingness to engage in a conversation that is alien to your life experience. A human instinct, which I have previously mentioned, is to shut down and immediately reject something that you don't agree with, that makes you feel uncomfortable, that jars with your perception and understanding of reality. This response, however, is not surprising given that rape is a taboo subject. The word itself evokes connotations of violence and brutality. Rape, the thought of it, the act of it, is widely abhorred across society and yet, when popular culture is saturated with misogyny and objectification, when the latest TikTok trend is popularised by thirteen-year-old girls mouthing misogynistic lyrics written by men joking about not wearing 'a johnny' if they 'beat it', when rape victims are intimidated into silence and warned that going to the police could ruin their rapist's life for ever, when hardcore porn is the place where teenagers learn how to have sex, porn that eroticises the degradation, objectification and violation of female bodies, when such porn is watched by MPs in the House of Commons, when fifty-six MPs stand accused of sexual misconduct, when the UK police force is found to be rife with a misogynistic culture where rape jokes are permissible on WhatsApp group chats, when prosecution rates for all rape cases is at an all-time low, effectively decriminalising rape in the UK; is rape really socially unacceptable?

Despite the evidence of the testimonies, the Ofsted review that confirmed the prevalence of sexual harassment and abuse online in all schools, and the thousands of young people that were speaking out and protesting in schools the phrase 'rape culture' was and still is controversial. We were surprised, after such resistance, to see it written in the headlines, being spoken about openly, and furiously discussed and picked apart by boys, girls, mums, dads, teachers, heads, MPs and police. The shock factor of the phrase galvanised the media, dominated the headlines and relentlessly sparked debates. The conversation kept going and going and going. As the issue remained at the top of the agenda for months, schools, universities, the police, and the government could no longer ignore it.

The arguments that were being used to attack Everyone's Invited were the same spurious arguments employed by the opponents of the #MeToo movement. Underlining them was an impetus to return the taboo subject of abuse to a place away from view, a place where we can pretend it doesn't exist. To brush it under the carpet to avoid a confrontation with one's own behaviour, an acknowledgement of behaviour you have actively participated in, behaviour that has contributed to a culture that enables and permits sexual violence. I understand this response as a human one, a primal instinct to survive, to remain in the bubble of safety, to be free from the ugliness and brutality of humanity. It is both painful and challenging to confront the scale and reality of sexual violence. In order to stay safe, unharmed, and untouched by pain many choose to distance themselves. This is how sexual abuse and violence continues to exist. When we dismiss, ignore, and continue in the face of suffering and abuse we maintain the status quo. This insidious cycle of violence remains hidden, allowed to thrive in our silence.

As a society, we must break this silence. We must continue uplifting these stories and listening to the experiences of survivors, we must continue having conversations. But we must also listen to, and attempt to understand and engage with the backlash. Backlash is part of the process. Yes, it's difficult to deal with and, yes, it's demoralising to receive, but it is also necessary. Backlash is a sobering reminder that this is only the beginning, there is still so much work left to be done. It is to be expected. And perhaps there is a lesson: that we need to listen to each other to make a change. In a world that's increasingly polarised, we must do all we can to find the empathy to relate to each other, to actively choose to listen to others and fight the instinct to immediately shut down when we hear something we disagree with. I keep thinking about the woman at the conference, and my response to her. Now with hindsight, I wish I had had the strength to sit down with her and listen to her story. Perhaps we would have found some common ground, perhaps she had sisters too, or grew up in a big city. Maybe, just maybe, if I had given her more of a chance, she would have given me one too.

Conclusion

In the past, when I have been attacked for my work, when the gravity of this suffering is questioned, I have felt an overwhelming energy pushing me onwards. I have felt an anger so deep, so intoxicating, that I wanted to stand on the edge of a cliff, driven by the voices, the generations of women throughout history, and SCREAM until my voice was hoarse. I wanted this scream to echo the trauma of thousands – millions – of girls and women who know pain, who live and embody it. Because to be a woman is to be in pain. And to be in pain is to be a woman.

It is the challenge of a lifetime to fight these urges. Where there is trauma there are layers of complicated emotions. The anger that many victims feel can be both a powerful and overwhelming affliction. Feeling anger as a survivor is justified. It is a human response. Yet anger can be blinding. Anger has the propensity for vengeance, vengeance that can too easily become a weapon. Those who choose to weaponise their victimhood, to inflict suffering on others, can very easily become the oppressors, the victim as the perpetrator – there are no more distinctions. If you choose to wield your power to inflict pain on others, your ideology will not redeem you. There is no justice in more suffering. Only more suffering.

In the days before I decided to share my experiences of harassment and abuse online, I had just finished watching Michaela Coel's TV series *I May Destroy You*. I found it to be a ground-breaking exploration of boundaries, sexual violence and trauma. The main characters were shown in their best and worst lights; they were layered, multidimensional individuals. They carried the capacity for good, kindness, and empathy but also the capacity to hurt, overpower and violate the boundaries of others. Watching these actors move seamlessly between the roles of victim, perpetrator and complicit bystander marked me profoundly, informing my approach in creating Everyone's Invited. It is crucial we understand one another as complex individuals, defined by our traumas *and* positive experiences. We all have the capacity to hurt others and, equally, we have a huge potential for goodness and love. This perspective on humanity requires empathy, which is the philosophical foundation for Everyone's Invited. Understanding how and why an individual comes to abuse another individual is essential to developing solutions to these problems. What is it about one's upbringing, their perspective on life and their beliefs that leads one person to dehumanise another? Arriving at this place of understanding and cultivating the empathy to get there is challenging.

When I first shared my own experiences, I was angry. As a survivor, as a friend to many survivors, and having read thousands of testimonies of sexual abuse and trauma, I know how easy it is to revel in this anger, to imagine perpetrators as monsters who are devoid of humanity and innately evil.

The stereotype of the lone rapist who lurks in dark alleys targeting their prey in the dead of night is all too familiar, but it is this sort of stereotype that feeds into the false assumption that rape is an extremely rare occurrence that is only committed by a mad, evil lunatic. This is not the case; the overwhelming majority of perpetrators of sexual violence are known to their victims. Rainn, the largest anti-sexual violence organisation in the US, reports that eight out of ten rapes are committed by someone the victim knows, whether they're a partner, spouse, friend, colleague or family member.[1] When we dismiss perpetrators as simply 'evil' we create distance and absolve ourselves from responsibility by erecting a clear barrier between the baddies and the goodies: Them versus Us. By doing this we create a sense of comfort, we feel safer because the 'evil' and the violence exists in a remote place, boxed up in the form of a 'monster' that has nothing to do with us. The reality is that sexual violence is a cultural issue that is sustained by all in society who fail to challenge the ideas, beliefs and behaviour that feed into a culture that enables real violence. We want to believe that the perpetrators are not like us or any of the people in our lives. But the truth is, they are.

Calling for empathy, forgiveness and compassion is a lot to ask of those who have suffered. Everyone's Invited has been on the receiving end of fierce criticism from our own community for encouraging empathy. But, ultimately, dehumanising perpetrators is not accountability and will not remedy the pervasive issue of sexual violence in society. bell hooks touched on these ideas, arguing that forgiveness and compassion are always linked. She asked her readers: 'how do we hold people accountable for wrongdoing and yet at the same time remain in touch with their humanity enough to believe in their capacity to be transformed?'[2]

We need to work with perpetrators to rehabilitate them. Doesn't everyone deserve the opportunity to change, to make amends, to apologise to their victim and to become accountable for their actions? When we *cancel* someone, we do not fix the cultural problem of sexual violence, we just remove it from view.

In the mainstreaming of hardcore pornography and in the digital revolution of the social world, never before has there been a greater gap between the lived experiences of the young and those of the old. Mine is the generation that has come of age at the turn of the century, and we have experienced a tremendous shift in the way we are living our lives: in the way we interact, access information, develop relationships and friendships, find love and have sex. In the digital landscape of the unknown, with little regulation, rules, guidance or control, archaic abuse has taken on new forms, which are alien to the generations before. In an age where social media platforms wield such power and influence, new challenges are emerging as the platforms evolve. Meta (Facebook) is launching the Metaverse, a virtual space where people who wear AR/ VR headsets can interact with each other's avatars, to play games, host meetings, go shopping, and on and on. Already, there are increasing reports of sexual harassment and intimidation from such interactions. These unregulated and unrestricted virtual spheres are becoming new homes to sexual predators.

Despite the shame and the stigma that shroud sex and incidents of sexual violence, over the past year thousands have bravely spoken out about their experiences. It is crucial that they are listened to; understanding the complex reality of sexual abuse, the impact of pornography, and the rise of digital-based violence and the many new forms of abuse on this spectrum, are vital, especially for the older generations who are the politicians, the educators, the judges, juries and parents. These experiences must not be dismissed. Yes, they are painful, yes, they are harrowing and, yes, they are triggering – but they cannot be ignored, brushed under the carpet and shut down as 'hysteria'. Frenzied political correctness and cancel culture may not always allow space for the mistakes and learning needed for genuine growth and positive change. But in the overwhelming majority of cases, young people are speaking out not because they're weak, sensitive, or 'woke warriors' who take offence easily; they are speaking out because they don't have a choice. This is about survival. This is a call for change because the state of the modern sexual landscape is dire, saturated with pornographic sexual scripts, abuse and the eroticisation of sexual violence. The movement for the right to call out sexual violence has grown for a multitude of reasons, including the right to live, to be, to exist, to survive, to have healthy relationships, to enjoy equal sexual pleasure, to go outside without the implicit threat of violence, to have sex freely and safely, to love. In her lifetime, Andrea Dworkin, the radical feminist who prophesied the ascent of Trump, the #MeToo movement, and the mainstreaming of hardcore pornography and its profound impact on the sex lives of the next generation of young people, was the target of visceral hatred from all corners of society, from her looks to her ideas. She was widely seen as a warning as to why women should not engage with radical feminism. After shouldering another attack from pro-pornography feminists in 1998, she lamented, 'I have a feeling that after my death I might be finally understood.' Just before her death in 2005, she reflected, 'Women will come back to feminism, because things are going to get far, far worse for us before they get better.'[3] Dworkin speaks nothing but the stone-cold truth as we are witnessing, in real time, the rights of women across the world being rolled back at an alarming rate. On 3 May 2022, a leak from the US Supreme Court suggested that the federal constitutional right to an abortion secured by Roe v Wade could be overturned. This would allow individual states in the US to set their own abortion laws, including outright bans.

In the digital world, behind closed doors and in the bedroom, women are increasingly facing a backwards, deeply misogynistic and abusive culture. One where men are entitled to sexual pleasure, where women give and do not receive, where pain is normalised in sex, where what is happening in mainstream hardcore porn is now happening in the real sex lives of teenagers. In the supposedly liberal and progressive West, there is an enormous gap between the rights that women have on paper versus their actual lived experiences of routine sexual harassment, misogyny, abuse, image-based abuse and sexual violence. Every girl and woman I know has had, at the very least, one experience on the spectrum of rape culture that has left them traumatised and changed in some way or another.

The act of writing this book has been transformative but at the same time it has been triggering. I have been forced to confront my own views, beliefs, experiences and values as I delved deeper into the reservoir of lived experiences, existing research, and studies in and around the topics I explore. It is painful to confront the scale of sexual violence, the root causes of this culture and how we've all allowed it to persist and thrive. There have been moments of pure shame and overwhelming paranoia as I considered my past experiences and the many mistakes I've made as a young person. Understanding why and how my own actions have caused harm to others is a challenging education in itself, but it is in this introspection that I encountered possibilities of correction, accountability and closure. Not only does this journey of introspection require courage, but a deep empathy, not just for those around us but also for ourselves.

I hope that as you reach my book's conclusion you have gained an understanding of the multifaceted, endlessly complex nature of these issues. As a child, I viewed the world through a binary and reductive lens, I didn't understand the unending variety of ways our childhoods and experiences and relationships inform the people we are today and the people we are becoming. I think there is a comfort in having the capacity to hold two contradictory ideas, and acknowledge that they can both exist and have meaning in equal measure. I now understand myself to be a person of mobility, finding comfort in a state of flux. I envision my life as a circle; I am a free agent who can move around the line, finding wisdom and guidance in the past as I study historical movements and change-makers, but I hope I am also someone with enough openness and empathy to embrace the present and look forward to the future, adjusting my thinking and values to find solutions to the experiences and problems of our time.

This circle is always turning, but the edges are soft and welcoming; all of it is connected. I want to learn from others who think differently, I want to evolve in my thinking. When there is so much suffering and it sometimes feels as if the world is burning at our feet, I look for hope and I believe it exists in connection, in togetherness, in the sharing and tolerance of each other's stories, ideas, identities and thoughts. In the end, what could be more important in life than human connection, a sense of community, solidarity, the strength gained in the deep knowing and understanding that you are not, and will never be, alone?

Acknowlededgments

This book and Everyone's Invited (EI) would not be possible without every single survivor who has bravely shared their story with us. Thank you for your courage, vulnerability, and honesty. It has been the privilege of a lifetime to amplify your stories and experience the blossoming of this beautiful community. Thank you to anyone and everyone who has supported us, whether it was sharing something online, speaking about it to your mum, listening to a friend share their story – in whatever way, big or small, you are part of this journey and the change.

From the inception of EI my dad, Kevin Sara, has wholeheartedly believed in and supported me at every stage of this journey. His contributions and commitment to the work and mission of EI have been integral to its growth and establishment. He is also my best friend, hero and role model whose lifelong values of kindness, empathy, perseverance, and balance have fundamentally shaped who I was, who I am, and who I strive to become.

Since the very beginning, EI has been driven forward by an extraordinary group of volunteers. One of the most rewarding things about this journey has been the friendships, connections and home that I've found amongst these individuals, and in particular, the founding members, who are, each with a unique skillset, bringing an essential piece of the puzzle to the table.

I would like to thank Wendy Mair who is the beating heart of Everyone's Invited. Thank you for teaching me to lead with compassion and to never stop having fun. Thank you for being unapologetic in what you believe in, for sticking to your guns, for inspiring us all, and for supporting EI with the best intentions and so much love. You are never ever bossy, only assertive!

I will forever be grateful for Arianne Obi who is one of my oldest friends and the first person I asked to help me set up an Instagram account called 'Everyone's Invited'. Your creativity, vision, selflessness and support over the past two years have been invaluable to EI and to me.

Ellie Softly, you are a superhero. I will forever be in awe of your kindness and steadfast support of others. Your support work for EI has been essential and means so much to every single volunteer. Thank you for looking after us, and for looking after me, thank you for weathering the storm and for always holding my hand!

I owe a great debt to the wonder who is Maddy Black. Thank you for your meticulous attention to detail, razor-sharp vision and distinctive voice. I am so grateful and unbelievably lucky to have you leading the way at EI. Thank you for your unwavering commitment, hard work and for sharing many special moments with me.

There is so much work that goes on behind the scenes and some of the most challenging tasks have been pioneered by the incredible Srivatsan (Chikku) Rajagopalan. Thank you Chikku for your open spirit, kindness, pragmatism, and willingness to learn.

Constanza Cecchetti is one of the brightest lights I know with an unstoppable commitment to building a better world. It's been such a pleasure to work with you and to call you a dear friend. Thank you for throwing yourself into EI and for your passion and care that goes into everything you do.

The early days were some of the most intense and emotionally stressful times. Charlotte Aldrich, thank you for your invaluable support and hard work. I will never forget our late-night phone calls and you tempering me in manic mode with your kindness and calming words.

I would like to extend my thanks to the following volunteers:

Lorcan Archibald
Dani Ball
Emily Chappell
Fleur De Bono
Maria Dimitriev
Lulu Goad

Livia Harper
Lucy Hewitson
Esther Huntington-Whiteley
Stela Kostomaj
Franciso Posada
Susie Reed
Iona Rowan
Katinka Rowland-Payne
Araminta Rowland-Payne
Alex Russell
Alexander Somers
Emma Tucker
Indira Verdding
Meadow Walker
Natasha Wilson

I am grateful for my editor, the wonderful Holly Harris who gave me this extraordinary opportunity, who believed in me and the work of EI from the very beginning. Holly's guidance, steady encouragement and empathy throughout this process has been crucial and formative to finding my voice as a first-time author. I will always cherish my time working with you, thank you for making this journey an unforgettable joy.

Thank you to the incredible Kaiya Shang who I had a wonderful time working so closely with throughout the editing stages. It is a rare privilege to work with someone who understands the nuances of my own experiences with such depth and compassion. Thank you for your incredible support, meticulous hard work, kind words and encouragement.

My eternal thanks to everyone at S&S who worked on this book: Polly Osborn, Rhiannon Carroll, Hannah Paget, Genevieve Barratt, Kat Ailes, Frances Jessop, Arzu Tahsin. I am also grateful to my amazing agents who have made this book a reality with their ceaseless championing and support: my thanks to Anna Dixon, Fiona Baird and Frankie Ali.

This book has been enriched by the knowledge I've gained from many individuals who I've had the pleasure and privilege to speak to over the past two years as part of my work for EI. Their generosity and openness in sharing their insights, knowledge and personal stories will always move me. From friends and family, to journalists, experts, educators, activists, academics, charities, frontline workers, police officers, teachers, heads, politicians, civil servants, parents, and young people. I also owe so much to the many books I've read by the legends of activism and feminism who have paved the way. Thank you especially to Evie Muir who I had the pleasure of interviewing and sharing some of her journey in this book.

My thanks to Olivia Cowley, one of my closest in this world, who kindly read some of the early essays and encouraged me to keep going and just write. I would also like to thank my dearest aunt, Elisabeth Kehoe, who was the first person to read the first draft of this book. Her overwhelming words of encouragement and advice moved me and gave me faith at a time where I had none. Her support and example will always mean so much to me as they have been instrumental in my development as a first-time author.

The reading, research, writing and editing of this book was completed in bedrooms, kitchens, living rooms, cafes and restaurants across London, Paris, and New York. I owe a great debt to each place, which holds a special significance in my life. Each city overflows with memories, conversations, moments, and friendships that have profoundly inspired and shaped this book.

My family are my most fundamental support system. My sisters, Cecelia and Vanessa, are the living and breathing reasons why I do the work that I do. Cecelia has always paved the way for me, thank you for being my biggest protector, supporter, and best friend. This book, my work, and the mission of EI has always been about creating a better world for the generations to come, I hope that my little sister will get to live in this world someday. I will be forever grateful for my trailblazing grandmother, Susan Sara, who has inspired me in her pioneering life and activism. Thank you for sharing your stories and thoughts with me, thank you for the many debates and conversations that we've had over dinners in Paris and long mountain walks. Thank you for housing and feeding me whilst I was completing the first draft. Sigal Shalev is an honorary member of the family who has given her time to EI as well as me, since I was very small. I am grateful for your thoughtfulness, deep care, and selfless support.

Acknowlededgments

I simply would not be without the force of female friendship in my life. I count my blessings every day that I am lucky enough to have grown up with the most incredible group of women who have relentlessly championed and supported me. Thank you from the bottom of my heart to the six loves of my life Katinka, Lindsay, Monike, Cowley, Cat and Saskia. As Cat once said, 'I know that wherever I go I will have the six of you holding me up on your shoulders and I'll never feel alone and forever feel loved'.

References

Introduction

1 Amia Srinivasan, *The Right to Sex* (London: Bloomsbury Publishing, 2021), p50
2 The British Academy, 'Leaders in SHAPE: Laura Bates' (26 April 2021), https://www.thebritishacademy.ac.uk/podcasts/leaders-in-shape-laura-bates/
3 *Guardian*, Today in Focus podcast, 'Men! What can you do to help fight misogyny' (24 March 2021), https://www.theguardian.com/news/audio/2021/mar/24/men-what-can-you-do-to-help-fight-misogyny-podcast
4 Michaela Coel, *Misfits* (New York: Henry Holt and Co., 2021), 93.

Beyond Gender Scripts

1 World Health Organization, 'Gender and Health', https://www.who.int/health-topics/gender#tab=tab_1
2 Sara L. Crawley and K. L. Broad, 'The Construction of Sex and Sexualities', in James Holstein and Jaber Gubrium, eds, *Handbook of Constructionist Research* (New York: Guilford Press, 2008), 545–66.
3 Teresa McDowell, *Applying Critical Social Theories to Family Therapy Practice* (New York: Springer, 2015).

4   American Psychological Association, *APA Dictionary of Psychology*, https://dictionary.apa.org/gender-script.

5   Moira Donegan, 'Part of the "great resignation" is actually just mothers forced to leave their jobs', *Guardian* (19 November 2021), https://www.theguardian.com/commentisfree/2021/nov/19/great-resignation-mothers-forced-to-leave-jobs

6   Paulette Light, 'Why 43% of Women With Children Leave Their Jobs, and How to Get Them Back', *The Atlantic* (19 April 2013), https://www.theatlantic.com/sexes/archive/2013/04/why-43-of-women-with-children-leave-their-jobs-and-how-to-get-them-back/275134/

7   Olivia Laing, 'The right to define yourself' in 'Human rights for the 21st century', *Guardian* (8 December 2018), https://www.theguardian.com/books/2018/dec/08/universal-declaration-human-rights-turns-70

8   Laing, 'The right to define yourself'.

9   Laing, 'The right to define yourself'.

10 Liam Stack, 'Overlooked No More: Karl Heinrich Ulrichs, Pioneering Gay Activist', *New York Times* (1 July 2020), https://www.nytimes.com/2020/07/01/obituaries/karl-heinrich-ulrichs-overlooked.html; 'Uranians', Encyclopedia.com, https://www.encyclopedia.com/social-sciences/encyclopedias-almanacs-transcripts-and-maps/uranians; 'Sexology', *Encyclopedia Britannica*, https://www.britannica.com/science/sexology

11 Sandra M. Gilbert, introduction to *Orlando* by Virgina Woolf (London: Penguin, 1993), xvii.

12 Eliot, T. S. (2021). *The Waste Land*. https://www.poetryfoundation.org/poems/47311/the-waste-land

Pain is Normal

1   Zadie Smith, *NW* (London: Hamish Hamilton, 2012), 33.

2   Katie Anthony, 'Is "Toxic Femininity" a Thing?', KatyKatiKate blog (19 December 2018), https://www.katykatikate.com/the-blog/2018/12/19/is-toxic-femininity-a-thing

3   Helen Block Lewis, *Shame and Guilt in Neurosis* (New York:

References

International Universities Press, 1971); Helen Block Lewis, 'Role of shame in depression in women' in R. Formanek and A. Gurian, eds, *Women and Depression: A lifespan perspective* (New York: Springer, 1987); Helen Block Lewis, ed., *The Role of Shame in Symptom Formation* (Hillsdale, NJ: Lawrence Erlbaum, 1987).

4 Michael Lewis, *Shame: The exposed self* (New York: The Free Press, 1992), 25..

5 Michael Lewis, *Shame*.

6 Anthony, 'Is "Toxic Femininity" a Thing?'

7 Lili Loofbouro, 'The Female Price of Male Pleasure', *The Week*, 25 January 2018, https://theweek.com/articles/749978/female-price-male-pleasure

8 Loofbouro, 'The Female Price of Male Pleasure',

9 Jessica Masterson, 'From beauty practices to sex, women and girls are conditioned to accept pain as necessary', Feminist Current (22 October 2019), https://www.feministcurrent.com/2019/10/22/from-beauty-practices-to-sex-women-and-girls-are-conditioned-to-accept-pain-as-necessary/

10 Peggy Orenstein, *Girls & Sex: Navigating the complicated new landscape* (New York: HarperCollins, 2016).

11 April Burns, Valerie A. Futch and Deborah L. Tolman, '"It's like doing homework": Academic achievement discourse in adolescent girls' fellatio narratives', *Sexuality Research & Social Policy: 8* (2011), 239–251, https://doi.org/10.1007/s13178-011-0062-1

12 Bahar Gholipour, 'Teen Anal Sex Study: 6 unexpected findings', *Live Science* (14 August 2014), https://www.livescience.com/47352-teen-anal-sex-unexpected-findings.html

13 Deborah Tolman in Orenstein, *Girls & Sex* 70.

14 Debby Herbenick in Orenstein, *Girls & Sex*, 71.

15 Loofbourow, 'The Female Price of Male Pleasure'.

16 Herbenick, in Orenstein, *Girls & Sex*, 71.

17 Kim Loliya in Gemma Askham, 'Why Do Women Put Up With Painful Sex?', BBC Three (20 April 2018), http://bbcthree-web-server.api.bbc.co.uk/bbcthree/article/db52efc3-c84c-4870-a4d0-f4ff183ec356

18 Sara I. McClelland, 'Intimate Justice: Sexual satisfaction in young adults', PhD dissertation, City University of New York, 2009.

19 Loofbourow, 'The Female Price of Male Pleasure'.

20 McClelland, 'Intimate Justice' in Loofbourow, 'The Female Price of Male Pleasure'.

21 Herbenick in Loofbourow, 'The Female Price of Male Pleasure'.

The Cost of Beauty

1 Janet Mock, 'Being pretty is a privilege, but we refuse to acknowledge it', allure (28 June 2017), https://www.allure.com/story/pretty-privilege

2 Lindsay Crouse, 'For Teen Girls, Instagram is a Cesspool', *New York Times* (8 October 2021), https://www.nytimes.com/2021/10/08/opinion/instagram-teen-girls-mental-health.html

3 Peggy Orenstein, *Girls & Sex: Navigating the complicated new landscape* (New York: HarperCollins, 2016), 18.

4 Orenstein, *Girls & Sex:* author's interview with Adriana Manago, Department of Psychology and Children's Digital Media Center, UCLA, 7 May 2010. See also Manago, Graham, Greenfield et al, 'Self-Presentation and Gender on MySpace'.

5 Orenstein, *Girls & Sex*, 19.

6 Pew Research Center, 'Mobile Fact Sheet' (7 April 2021), https://www.pewresearch.org/internet/fact-sheet/mobile/

7 PA Media, 'Most children own mobile phone by age of seven, study finds', *Guardian* (30 January 2020), https://www.theguardian.com/society/2020/jan/30/most-children-own-mobile-phone-by-age-of-seven-study-finds

8 Derek Thompson, 'Social Media is Attention Alcohol', *Atlantic* (17 September 2021), https://www.theatlantic.com/ideas/archive/2021/09/social-media-attention-alcohol-booze-instagram-twitter/620101/

9 Royal Society for Public Health, #StatusOfMind: Social media and young people's mental health and wellbeing (May 2017), https://www.rsph.org.uk/static/uploaded/d125b27c-0b62-41c5-a2c0155a8887cd01.pdf

10 Georgia Wells, Jeff Horowitz and Deepa Seetharaman, 'Facebook Knows Instagram is Toxic for Teen Girls, Company Documents Show', *Wall Street Journal* (14 September 2021), https://www.

wsj.com/articles/facebook-knows-instagram-is-toxic-for-teen-girls-company-documents-show-11631620739

11 Damien Gayle, 'Facebook aware of Instagram's harmful effect on teenage girls, leak reveals', *Guardian* (14 September 2021), https://www.theguardian.com/technology/2021/sep/14/facebook-aware-instagram-harmful-effect-teenage-girls-leak-reveals

12 Farahnaz Mohammed, 'Our ugly obsession with beauty', Girls' Globe (16 August 2013), https://www.girlsglobe.org/2013/08/16/our-ugly-obsession-with-beauty/

The Best Men Can Be

1 'Gillette #MeToo razors ad on "toxic masculinity" gets praise – and abuse', *Guardian*, 15 January 2019, https://www.theguardian.com/world/2019/jan/15/gillette-metoo-ad-on-toxic-masculinity-cuts-deep-with-mens-rights-activists

2 Piers Morgan, Twitter (14 January 2019), https://twitter.com/piersmorgan/status/1084891133757587456?ref_src=twsrc%5Etfw%7Ctwcamp%5Etweetembed%7Ctwterm%5E1084891133757587456%7Ctwgr%5E%7Ctwcon%5Es1_&ref_url=https%3A%2F%2Fwww.theguardian.com%2Fworld%2F2019%2Fjan%2F15%2Fgillette-metoo-ad-on-toxic-masculinity-cuts-deep-with-mens-rights-activists

3 Andrew P Street, Twitter (15 January 2019), https://twitter.com/AndrewPStreet/status/1084991818029137921?ref_src=twsrc%5Etfw%7Ctwcamp%5Etweetembed%7Ctwterm%5E1084991818029137921%7Ctwgr%5E%7Ctwcon%5Es1_&ref_url=https%3A%2F%2Fwww.theguardian.com%2Fworld%2F2019%2Fjan%2F15%2Fgillette-metoo-ad-on-toxic-masculinity-cuts-deep-with-mens-rights-activists

4 Alexandra Topping, Kate Lyons and Matthew Weaver, 'Gillette #MeToo razors ad on "toxic masculinity" gets praise – and abuse', *Guardian* (15 January 2019), https://www.theguardian.com/world/2019/jan/15/gillette-metoo-ad-on-toxic-masculinity-cuts-deep-with-mens-rights-activists

5 bell hooks, *The Will to Change: Men, masculinity, and love* (New York: Atria Books, 2004), 66.

6   Rainn, 'Sexual assault of men and boys', https://www.rainn.org/
    articles/sexual-assault-men-and-boys

7   Office for National Statistics, Crime Survey for England and
    Wales and police recorded crime, 'Sexual Offences Victim
    Characteristics, England and Wales: year ending March 2020',
    (18 March 2021), https://www.ons.gov.uk/peoplepopulation
    andcommunity/crimeandjustice/articles/sexualoffencesvictim
    characteristicsenglandandwales/march2020#sex

8   Mankind UK, 'Mankind UK Research Feb 21', (February 2021),
    https://www.1in6.uk/unwanted-sexual-experiences/the-1-in-6-statistic/

9   Office for National Statistics, 'Suicides in England and Wales:
    2020 registrations' (7 September 2021), https://www.ons.gov.uk/
    peoplepopulationandcommunity/birthsdeathsandmarriages/deaths/
    bulletins/suicidesintheunitedkingdom/2020registrations

10 'Nudes, porn, abuse – the toxic culture in UK classrooms',
    The Times, 15 April 2021 https://www.thetimes.co.uk/article/
    nudes-porn-abuse-the-toxic-culture-in-uk-classrooms-fl3m
    7wjmg

11 Dearbhla Crosse, 'The language we use allows misogynists like
    Wayne Couzens to go unchecked', *Independent* (1 October
    2021), https://www.independent.co.uk/voices/wayne-couzens-
    rapist-language-misogyny-b1930520.html

12 Dearbhla Crosse, 'The language we use allows misogynists like
    Wayne Couzens to go unchecked', *Independent* (1 October
    2021), https://www.independent.co.uk/voices/wayne-couzens-
    rapist-language-misogyny-b1930520.html

13 David Batty, 'Research reveals rapes and assaults admitted to by
    male UK students', *Guardian* (29 October 2021), https://www.
    theguardian.com/society/2021/oct/29/research-reveals-rapes-
    and-assaults-admitted-to-by-male-uk-students

14 Batty, 'Research reveals rapes and assaults admitted to by male
    UK students'.

15 Batty, 'Research reveals rapes and assaults admitted to by male
    UK students'.

16 Crosse, 'The language we use allows misogynists like Wayne
    Couzens to go unchecked', *Independent*.

17 Femicide Census, press release, 'Men still killing one woman
    every three days in UK – It is time for "Deeds not Words"'

(28 February 2022), https://www.femicidecensus.org/men-still-killing-one-woman-every-three-days-in-uk-we-need-deeds-not-words/

18 Glennon Doyle, *Untamed: Stop Pleasing, Start Living* (London: Penguin Random House 2020), 169.

I Feel You Watching

1 Brian Hiatt, 'Adele: Inside Her Private Life and Triumphant Return', *Rolling Stone*, 3 November 2015, https://www.rollingstone.com/music/music-features/adele-inside-her-private-life-and-triumphant-return-37131/

2 James Rodger, 'Adele looks slimmer than ever after weight loss in fresh update', *Birmingham Live* (7 January 2022), https://www.birminghammail.co.uk/news/showbiz-tv/adele-looks-slimmer-ever-after-22680913

3 Jane McGuire, '5 tips we can learn from Adele's amazing weight loss', Tom's Guide (23 January 2022), https://www.tomsguide.com/uk/news/5-things-we-can-all-learn-from-adeles-exercise-routine

4 Chloe Wilt, 'Adele's Holiday Photos Spark Debate on Weight Loss', CafeMom (27 December 2019), https://cafemom.com/entertainment/adele-photos-weight-debate

5 Shannon Pauls, 'I'm a Little Bummed That Adele Lost Weight', *Slate* (15 October 2021), https://slate.com/human-interest/2021/10/adele-weight-loss-im-a-little-upset.html

6 Sarra Gray, 'Adele weight loss: Singer shows off staggering transformation in new snap', *Express* (14 July, 2021, updated 18 July 2021), https://www.express.co.uk/life-style/diets/1461442/weight-loss-adele-diet-plan-2021-latest-pictures

7 Rebecca Solnit, *Wanderlust: A history of walking* (London: Granta, 2014), 235.

8 Solnit, *Wanderlust*, 234.

9 Solnit, *Wanderlust*, 235.

10 Solnit, *Wanderlust*, 240.

11 Solnit, *Wanderlust*, 240.

Objects

1 Amia Srinivasan, *The Right to Sex* (London: Bloomsbury Publishing, 2021), 50.

2 Peggy Orenstein, *Girls & Sex: Navigating the complicated new landscape* (New York: HarperCollins, 2016), 26.

3 John Berger, *Ways of Seeing* (London: Penguin Classics 2008)

4 Berger, *Ways of Seeing*, 47.

5 Laura Mulvey/Rachel Rose, 'Visual Pleasure and Narrative Cinema', (London: Afterall Books, 2016).

6 Amélie Pavel, 'You Are Your Own Voyeur: Female Sexualiy and the Male Gaze', programme notes, doc films, https://docfilms.uchicago.edu/dev/calendar/fall2018/thursdays1.shtml

7 Orenstein, *Girls & Sex*, 27–8.

8 Emily Ratajkowski, *My Body* (London: Quercus, 2021), 30–35.

9 Orenstein, *Girls & Sex*, 27–8.

10 Orenstein, *Girls & Sex*.

11 https://www.washingtonpost.com/opinions/2022/03/17/sex-ethics-rethinking-consent-culture/ ; https://www.nytimes.com/2022/03/21/opinion/manifesto-against-sex-positivity.html

12 Ariel Levy, *Female Chauvinist Pigs: Women and the rise of raunch culture* [ebook] (London: Simon & Schuster UK, 2014), eBook.

13 Levy, *Female Chauvinist Pigs*.

14 Amanda McCracken, 'Is the Next Phase of Sex Positivity Choosing Not to Have Sex?', *Vogue*, 9 April 2022, https://www.vogue.com/article/sex-positivity-late-in-life-virginity

15 Amanda McCracken, 'Is the next phase of sex positivity choosing not to have sex?', *Vogue* (9 April 2022), quoting psychologist and Stanford lecturer Meag-gan O-Reilly.

16 Orenstein, *Girls & Sex*, 43.

17 Thirst trap: a social media post intended to entice people sexually.

18 Simone de Beauvoir, *The Second Sex*, trans. Howard M. Parshley (London: Jonathan Cape, 1953).

19 de Beauvoir, *The Second Sex*.

References

Just a Joke

1 https://aeon.co/ideas/how-playing-wittgensteinian-language-games-can-set-us-free

2 Linda Coates and Allan Wade, 'Telling it Like it Isn't: Obscuring Perpetrator Responsibility for Violent Crime, *Discourse and Society*, 15(5) (September 2004), 499–526. doi: 10.1177/0957926504045031

3 Brené Brown, 'Dehumanizing Always Starts With Language', Brenebrown.com (17 May 2018), https://brenebrown.com/articles/2018/05/17/dehumanizing-always-starts-with-language/

4 Monica Romero-Sánchez, Hugo Carretero-Dios, Jesus L. MEgias, Miguel Moya and Thomas E. Ford, 'Sexist humor and rape proclivity: The moderating role of joke teller gender and severity of sexual assault', *Violence Against Women* 23(8) (July 2017), 951–972, https://gap.hks.harvard.edu/sexist-humor-and-rape-proclivity-moderating-role-joke-teller-gender-and-severity-sexual-assault

5 T. E. Ford, 'Effects of sexist humor on tolerance of sexist events', *Personality and Social Psychology Bulletin*, 26 (1 November 2000), 1094–1107, https://doi.org/10.1177/01461672002611006

6 T. E. Ford, C. F. Boxer, J. Armstrong, J. R. Edel, 'More Than "Just a Joke": The Prejudice-Releasing Function of Sexist Humor', *Personality and Social Psychology Bulletin*, 34 (February 2008),159–170, https://doi.org/10.1177/0146167207310022

7 T. E. Ford, J. A. Woodzicka, S. R. Triplett and A. O. Kochersberger, 'Sexist humor and beliefs that justify societal sexism', *Current Research in Social Psychology*, 21 (January 2013), 64–81, https://www.researchgate.net/publication/286382131_Sexist_humor_and_beliefs_that_justify_societal_sexism

8 M. Romero-Sánchez, et al, 'Sexist Humor and Rape Proclivity: The Moderating Role of Joke Teller Gender and Severity of Sexual Assault', *Violence Against Women* (article first published online 6 July 2016), 23(8) (1 July 2017), 951–72. doi: 10.1177/1077801216654017

9 https://citedatthecrossroads.net/fys05/2013/10/16/rewatching-superbad-point-of-view-the-gaze-and-formal-analysis/

10 George the Poet, https://www.georgethepoet.com/podcast-library, Episode 1

11 'Jermaine Goupall: Four jailed over Croydon gang murder', BBC News, 15 February 2018, https://www.bbc.co.uk/news/uk-england-london-43076017; 'YouTube is still hosting Jermaine Goupall killer M-Trap's drill videos', *The Times*, 3 June 2018, https://www.thetimes.co.uk/article/youtube-is-still-hosting-jermaine-goupall-killer-m-traps-drill-videos-zqbv2b6dv

12 Ciaran Thapar, 'Don't censor drill music, listen to what it's trying to tell us', *Guardian* (6 February 2019), https://www.theguardian.com/commentisfree/2019/feb/06/dont-censor-drill-music-listen-skengdo-am?curator=MusicREDEF

13 Olivia B. Waxman, '"Baby It's Cold Outside" Was Controversial From the Beginning. Here's What to Know About Consent in the 1940s', *Time* (5 December 2019, updated 23 December 2020), https://time.com/5739183/baby-its-cold-outside-consent/

14 Ann Powers, 'When Pop Stars Flirt With Bad Taste', NPR (The Record) (3 July 2013), https://www.npr.org/sections/therecord/2013/07/02/198097817/the-record-when-pop-stars-flirt-with-danger?t=1651702189074

15 Annie Zaleski, 'Robin Thicke Blurred Lines', *A.V. Club* (30 July 2013), https://www.avclub.com/robin-thicke-blurred-lines-1798177514

16 Keith Harris, 'Robin Thicke's "Blurred Lines" Is the Album Justin Timberlake Was Too Famous to Make', *Spin* (29 July 2013), https://www.spin.com/2013/07/robin-thicke-blurred-lines-justin-timberlake/

Ubiquitous Porn and Naïve Parents

1 Bernardine Evaristo, *Girl, Woman, Other* (London: Hamish Hamilton, 2019), 52–3.

2 Similarweb, 'Top Websites Ranking for Adult in the world', https://www.similarweb.com/top-websites/category/adult/

3 '2019 Year in Review', Pornhub Insights, Pornhub (11 December 2019), https://www.pornhub.com/insights/2019-year-in-review

4 Norman Doidge, *The Brain that Changes Itself: Stories of personal triumph from the frontiers of brain science* (London: Penguin Books, 2008).

5 'Billie Eilish says watching porn as a child "destroyed my brain"', *Guardian*,15 December 2021, https://www.theguardian.com/music/2021/dec/15/billie-eilish-says-watching-porn-gave-her-nightmares-and-destroyed-my-brain; 'Billie Eilish says porn exposure while young caused her nightmares', 14 December 2021, BBC News, https://www.bbc.co.uk/news/entertainment-arts-59658663

6 Janice Turner, 'Porn apologists are running out of excuses', *The Times* (17 December 2021), https://www.thetimes.co.uk/article/porn-apologists-are-running-out-of-excuses-rzxrs3087

7 Janice Turner, 'Porn apologists are running out of excuses', *The Times* (17 December 2021), https://www.thetimes.co.uk/article/porn-apologists-are-running-out-of-excuses-rzxrs3087

8 Peggy Orenstein, *Girls & Sex*: Navigating the complicated new landscappe (New York: Harpercollins, 2016), 35: personal interview, Bryant Paul, Indiana University Bloomington, 4 December 2014.

9 Nick Hillman, 'Sex and Relationships Among Students: Summary Report', Higher Education Policy Institute, April 2021.

10 '2021 Year in Review', Pornhub Insights, Pornhub (14 December 2021), https://www.pornhub.com/insights/yir-2021#Categorical-Analysis

11 Hillman, 'Sex and Relationships Among Stuidents'.

12 David Sanderson, 'Playground Sex Assaults "Are Becoming an Epidemic"', *The Times* (12 August 2018), https://www.thetimes.co.uk/article/playground-sex-assaults-are-becoming-an-epidemic-wcxh63tll

13 Alys Harte, ' "A man tried to choke me during sex without warning"', BBC News (28 November 2019), https://www.bbc.co.uk/news/uk-50546184

14 We Can't Consent To This, 'Who Claims "Sex Games Gone Wrong"' (3 July 2019, updated 19 November 2019), https://wecantconsenttothis.uk/blog/2019/7/3/who-uses-this-defence

15 Sophie Gallagher, 'Third of British Women Have Experienced Unwanted Choking, Slapping or Spitting During Sex', *Independent*, 28 November 2019, https://www.independent.co.uk/life-style/women/women-choking-slapping-spitting-sex-abuse-violence-survey-a9222841.html

16 Briony Smith, 'The Shocking Sex Trend That Will Leave You Breathless', *Flare* (9 February 2017), https://www.flare.com/celebrity/entertainment/waiting-to-exhale-breathplay/

17 Niki Fritz, Vinny Malic, Bryant Paul and Yanyan Zhou, 'A Descriptive Analysis of the Types, Targets, and Relative Frequency of Aggression in Mainstream Pornography', *Archives of Sexual Behavior*, 49, no.8 (November 2020), 3041–3053, https://doi.org/10.1007/s10508-020-01773-0

18 Anonymous, '"Our kids were raped by classmates. the DfE won't listen"', *The Times Educational Supplement* (13 September 2018), https://www.tes.com/magazine/news/general/our-kids-were-raped-classmates-dfe-wont-listen

19 Amia Srinivasan, *The Right to Sex* (London: Bloomsbury Publishing, 2021), 41.

20 Srinivasan, *The Right to Sex*, 40.

21 Gert Martin Hald, Neil M. Malamuth and Carlin Yuen, 'Pornography and Attitudes Supporting Violence Against Women: Revisiting the relationship in nonexperimental studies', *Aggressive Behavior*, 36, no.1 (January/February 2010), 18, https://doi.org/10.1002/ab.20328

22 Neil M. Malamuth, Tamara Addison and Mary Koss, 'Pornography and Sexual Aggression: Are there reliable effects and can we understand them?', *Annual Review of Sex Research*, 11 (February 2000), 26–91, https://www.tandfonline.com/doi/abs/10.1080/10532528.2000.10559784

23 Joetta L. Carr and Karen M. VanDeusen, 'Risk Factors for Male Sexual Aggression on College Campuses', *Journal of Family Violence*, 19, no.5 (October 2004), 279–89, https://doi.org/10.1023/B:JOFV.0000042078.55308.4d

24 Elizabeth Oddone-Paolucci, Mark Genuis and Claudio Violato, 'A Meta-Analysis of the Published Research on the Effects of Pornography', *The Changing Family and Child Development* (London: Routledge, 2000), 48–59.

25 Matthew W. Brosi, John D. Foubert, R. Sean Bannon and Gabriel Yandell, 'Effects of Sorority Members' Pornography Use on Bystander Intervention in a Sexual Assault Situation and Rape Myth Acceptance', *Oracle: The Research Journal of the*

Association of Fraternity/Sorority Advisors, 6, no.2 (September 2011), 26–35, https://doi.org/10.25774/60dk-dg51

26 Paul J. Wright and Michelle Funk, 'Pornography Consumption and Opposition to Affirmative Action for Women: A prospective study', *Psychology of Women Quarterly*, 38, no.2 (May 2013), 208–21, https://doi.org/10.1177/0361684313 498853

27 Srinivasan, *The Right to Sex*, 42.

28 MacKinnon, *Only Words* (Harvard University Press, 1996 [1993]), 19-20.

29 MacKinnon, *Only Words*, 19–20.

The Collectors

1 These gender norms were listed by Debbie Ging, Associate Professor of Digital Media and Gender in the School of Communications, at the event described in this essay to launch the UCL report, 'Understanding and Combatting Youth Experiences of Image-Based Sexual Harassment and Abuse' (December 2021).

2 Debbie Ging, speaking at the launch of the UCL report.

3 Jessica Ringrose, Kaitlyn Regehr and Betsy Milne, 'Understanding and Combatting Youth Experiences of Image-Based Sexual Harassment and Abuse' (Leicester: Association of School and College Leaders, December 2021), https://www.ascl. org.uk/ASCL/media/ASCL/Our%20view/Campaigns/ Understanding-and-combatting-youth-experiences-of-image-based-sexual-harassment-and-abuse-full-report.pdf

4 Clare McGlynn and Kelly Johnson, 'Criminalising Cyberflashing: Options for law reform', *The Journal of Criminal Law* 85, no.3 (June 2021), 171–188, https://doi.org/10.1177/ 0022018320972306

5 Ringrose et al, 'Understanding and Combatting Youth Experiences of Image-Based Sexual Harassment and Abuse'.

6 Ringrose et al, 'Understanding and Combatting Youth Experiences of Image-Based Sexual Harassment and Abuse'.

7 Ringrose et al, 'Understanding and Combatting Youth Experiences of Image-Based Sexual Harassment and Abuse'.

8 Ringrose et al, 'Understanding and Combatting Youth Experiences of Image-Based Sexual Harassment and Abuse'.

9 Ofsted, 'Review of sexual abuse in schools and colleges' (10 June 2021), https://www.gov.uk/government/publications/review-of-sexual-abuse-in-schools-and-colleges/review-of-sexual-abuse-in-schools-and-colleges

10 Ofsted, 'Review of sexual abuse in schools and colleges'.

11 https://www.gov.uk/government/publications/joint-committee-report-on-the-draft-online-safety-bill-government-response/government-response-to-the-joint-committee-report-on-the-draft-online-safety-bill

12 'Online Safety Bill: New offences and tighter rules', BBC News, 14 December 2021, https://www.bbc.co.uk/news/technology-59638569.

13 UK Parliament, Committees, 'No longer the land of the lawless: Joint Committee reports' (14 December 2021), https://committees.parliament.uk/committee/534/draft-online-safety-bill-joint-committee/news/159784/no-longer-the-land-of-the-lawless-joint-committee-reports/

14 Ringrose et al, 'Understanding and Combatting Youth Experiences of Image-Based Sexual Harassment and Abuse' 60.

Nothing Compares to an English Rose

1 Katherine Cross, 'To some white men . . .' [Twitter post], 2.41 a.m., 4 May 2018, https://twitter.com/Quinnae_Moon/status/992217692651360256

2 Amia Srinivasan, *The Right to Sex* (London: Bloomsbury Publishing, 2021), 103.

3 Carolyn M. West and Kalimah Johnson, 'Sexual Violence in the Lives of African American Women', National Online Resource Center on Violence Against Women (March 2013), http://dx.doi.org/10.13140/2.1.3850.9444

4 Sistah Space, 'Valerie's Law', https://www.sistahspace.org/valerieslaw

5 Hannah Summers, 'Police Urged to Better Protect Black Women Who Face Domestic Abuse', *Guardian*, 15 September 2021,

References

https://www.theguardian.com/society/2021/sep/15/police-urged-to-better-protect-black-women-who-face-domestic-abuse

6 Sir William Macpherson of Cluny, 'Stephen Lawrence Inquiry' report (February 1999), https://assets.publishing.service.gov.uk/government/uploads/system/uploads/attachment_data/file/277111/4262.pdf, 6.34

7 Reni Eddo-Lodge, *Why I'm No Longer Talking to White People About Race* (London: Bloomsbury Circus, 2018), 156.

8 bell hooks, *Ain't I a Woman: Black women and feminism* (London: Taylor & Francis, 2014).

9 bell hooks, *Ain't I a Woman: Black women and feminism* (London: Taylor & Francis, 2014).

10 Amia Srinivasan, *The Right to Sex* (London: Bloomsbury Publishing, 2021), 170

11 Srinivasan, *The Right to Sex*, 17.

Movements Making Movements

1 Rebecca Solnit, *Wanderlust: A history of walking* (London: Granta, 2014), 242.

2 Katy Waldman, 'A Sociologist Examines the "White Fragility" That Prevents White Americans from Confronting Racism', *New Yorker* (23 July 2018), https://www.newyorker.com/books/page-turner/a-sociologist-examines-the-white-fragility-that-prevents-white-americans-from-confronting-racism

3 Waldman, 'A Sociologist Examines'.

Backlash

1 Damian Whitworth, 'The Everyone's Invited scandal: what happened next,' *The Times*, 20 June 2022, https://www.thetimes.co.uk/article/everyones-invited-scandal-what-happened-next-soma-sara-gkf77smlh

2 Melanie McDonagh, 'Teenage life has never been so fraught', *Spectator* (27 March 2021), https://www.spectator.co.uk/article/everyones-invited-shows-that-nobodys-safe

3 Jess Zimmerman, 'Not All Men: A Brief History of Every Dude's Favorite Argument', *Time* (28 April 2014), https://time.

com/79357/not-all-men-a-brief-history-of-every-dudes-favorite-argument/

4 Marie-Claire Chappet, 'Why do we protect promising young men over promising young women?', *Harper's Bazaar* (12 April 2021), https://www.harpersbazaar.com/uk/culture/a35519409/promising-young-woman-comment/

5 'Dozens of letters urge leniency for Brock Turner in Stanford sexual assault case', *Guardian*, 7 June 2016, https://www.theguardian.com/us-news/2016/jun/07/stanford-sexual-assault-letters-brock-turner-judge

6 https://www.espn.com/college-sports/story/_/id/15938889/brock-turner-former-stanford-cardinal-swimmer-sentenced-six-months-jail

7 'Here's The Powerful Letter The Stanford Victim Read To Her Attacker', Katie J.M. Baker, *Buzzfeed*, 3 June 2016, https://www.buzzfeednews.com/article/katiejmbaker/heres-the-powerful-letter-the-stanford-victim-read-to-her-ra

8 'Transcript: Donald Trump's Taped Comments About Women', *New York Times*, 8 October 2016, https://www.nytimes.com/2016/10/08/us/donald-trump-tape-transcript.html

9 Michaela Coel, *Misfits: A Personal Manifesto* (New York: Henry Holt and Co., 2021), 87.

10 https://www.theguardian.com/society/2020/jul/17/one-in-70-recorded-rapes-in-england-and-wales-led-to-charge-last-year; https://www.thetimes.co.uk/article/rape-claims-soar-but-charges-hit-record-low-xnp627p8m

11 'Nous défendons une liberté d'importuner, indispensable à la liberté sexuelle', Le Monde, 9 January 2018, https://www.lemonde.fr/idees/article/2018/01/09/nous-defendons-une-liberte-d-importuner-indispensable-a-la-liberte-sexuelle_5239134_3232.html

12 'Nous défendons une liberté d'importuner, indispensable à la liberté sexuelle', Le Monde, 9 January 2018, https://www.lemonde.fr/idees/article/2018/01/09/nous-defendons-une-liberte-d-importuner-indispensable-a-la-liberte-sexuelle_5239134_3232.html

Conclusion

1 Rainn, 'Perpetrators of Sexual Violence: Statistics', https://www.rainn.org/statistics/perpetrators-sexual-violence
2 Melvin McLeod, '"There's No Place to Go But Up" – bell hooks and Maya Angelou in conversation', *Lion's Roar* (1 January 1998), www.lionsroar.com/theres-no-place-to-go-but-up/
3 Julie Bindel, 'Why Andrea Dworkin is the radical, visionary feminist we need in our terrible times', *Guardian* (16 April 2019), https://www.theguardian.com/lifeandstyle/2019/apr/16/why-andrea-dworkin-is-the-radical-visionary-feminist-we-need-in-our-terrible-times

Index

Index